What people are saying

- "Extremely knowledgeable, personable and genuine. I would thoroughly recommend working with Paul"

- "Paul is an invaluable growth partner, and one of the most supportive people I know"

- "Provides real life examples based on his experience that links theory to practice".

- "Paul has been an excellent Chair and oversees the extensive work of the Board effectively"

- "We will never thank you enough for what you done for us"

- "Paul is a highly competent PM consultant who can absorb business concepts and manage complex projects"

- "Clearly results driven, methodical and excellent communication skills."

- "His expert knowledge allowed him to monitor and oversee a number of projects ensuring they were delivered on time and to a high standard"

About the Author

Paul Taylor is a Consultant with over 30 years' experience of implementing change across the financial services, oil/gas, charities and professional bodies.

Author and speaker on a variety of subjects (such as Change, freelancing, technology, financial services, research approaches plus others).

Published several books covering Financial Services, Technology, Contracting and Change.

Chair and NED for a variety of industry and social enterprises Mentor to various people on areas on career planning, career changes, etc.

Associate Lecturer for the Open University STEM School teaching Technology Management.

Obtained an MBA from the Open University.

Table of Contents

	Acknowledgements	13
1	Introduction	14
2	**Definitions**	17
2.1	Introduction	17
2.2	What is change?	17
2.3	What is a programme, a project, a portfolio or a change?	18
2.4	For clarity and ease of reading, this book will use the term "Change" to cover Projects, Programmes and Portfolios.	22
2.5	What is change Management?	22
3	**The reasons for change failure**	s24
3.1	Introduction	24
3.2	What are the seven factors that help and/or hinder change within organisations?	24
4	**Does the organisation have the skills and capabilities to implement Change successfully?**	30
4.1	Introduction	30
	INTERNAL ISSUES	32
4.2	Has the organisation grown by acquisition?	32
4.3	How much autonomy from the parent does the organisation have?	34
4.4	How silo'ed is the organisation?	35

4.5	How well is the Missions Statement and Strategic Direction understood?	37
4.6	How well does the organisation react to Market and Industry changes?	39
4.7	How much customer focus does the organisation have?	40
4.8	How well does the organisation learn from their mistakes?	42
4.9	How much empowerment do staff have to make decisions?	44
4.10	How supportive and knowledgeable are senior management?	46
4.11	How well does the organisation's culture manage the human aspects?	48
4.12	Does the organisations have an organisation-wide committee to oversee all changes that are either planned or in progress?	51
4.13	Does the organisations have an organisation-wide Change Management process that can be used for all Changes that need to be made?	54
4.14	Does the organisations have an organisation-wide Change Control process to manage changes in scope, timelines, etc. for inflight changes?	56
4.15	Are the various Change Management processes a good 'cultural' fit for the organisation?	58
4.16	What should an organisation do if they do not have any for insufficient Change Management processes?	59
4.17	How susceptible is the organisation to the latest management and/or change 'fads'?	61
EXTERNAL ISSUES		63
4.18	How regulated is the environment that the organisation operates in?	63
4.19	How complex is the client base?	65

4.20	How complex is the set of products and/or services offered?	67
	HYBRID INTERNAL AND EXTERNAL ISSUES	70
4.21	How well is the operating model understood?	70
4.22	It is important to ensure that consistent terminology is used across all stakeholders.	74

5	**Has sufficient pre-planning work been performed?**	**76**
5.1	Introduction	76
	INITIAL THINKING	79
5.2	Is it clear what has triggered the change?	79
5.3	Is it clear what the business case for the change is?	81
5.4	Is it clear who will benefit from the change?	84
5.5	Is there a clearly defined and agreed set of success criteria?	85
5.6	Is there a clear vision of the end-state (or what the world will look like once the change is implemented)?	88
5.7	Is there an understanding of what the Business Requirements for the Change are?	90
5.8	Has a suitable amount of money been allocated to the change?	95
5.9	Does the organisation understand the complexity of the change being implemented?	98
5.10	All changes will have a large number of problems and the stakeholders must be aware of this?	100
	PLANNING	102
5.11	Is there an understanding of what 'things' need to be changed to implement the change?	102

5.12	Is there an understanding of how the change will be transitioned into the live environment?	104
5.13	Has an initial change plan (even if draft) been completed?	106

GOVERNANCE 110

5.14	Does the change have an appropriate Sponsor?	110
5.15	Is there suitable senior management oversight and forums in place?	112
5.16	Is there a suitable Change Manager in place?	114
5.17	Is there an appropriate communication strategy in place?	117
5.18	Have suitable processes and controls been implemented?	119
5.19	Have all issues, ambiguities and gaps have been logged at the start of the change?	120

WHO NEEDS TO BE INVOLVED AS PART OF THE CHANGE TEAM 122

5.20	Is it clear what people, teams and organisations need to be involved in implementing the change	122
5.21	Is there a suitable works stream structure in place to ensure the change is delivered?	124
5.22	Have the required internal staff been included in the Change Team?	126
5.23	Does the organisation have the required skill sets in place?	127
5.24	Have all the required external suppliers being engaged in the change	128
5.25	Have the required Internal or intragroup suppliers being engaged in the change	130
5.26	Have all required customers been engaged in the change?	131

5.27	Has the required infrastructure for the change been put in place?	133
	SAY THANK YOU	135
5.28	Is the Change Team being appreciated for their work and efforts?	135
6	**Is the change being implemented in the most appropriate manner?**	**137**
6.1	Introduction	137
6.2	How supportive and knowledgeable are senior management?	138
6.3	How well are the Change Manager and the Sponsor working together?	140
6.4	Are the correct number of issues being raised for the size of the change?	141
6.5	Does the change 'feel' like is progressing well?	142
6.6	How well are change issues and problems being managed?	144
6.7	Are Change Team members working constantly long hours?	145
6.8	Is the governance structure in place still fit-for-purpose now the change is up and running?	147
6.9	Are key decisions being made as and when they are needed?	149
6.10	How well is resistance being identified and managed during the change?	152
6.11	How much re-planning is taking place during implementation?	156
6.12	How effective is the stakeholder communication strategy?	157

6.13	Are stakeholders hearing about problems with the Change from people outside the Change Team?	159
6.14	How well are the external suppliers being managed?	162
6.15	How well are intragroup or internal suppliers being managed?	166
6.16	How effectively are customers being managed?	169
6.17	How well are the human aspects of the change being managed?	173
6.18	Remember that all changes will have issues and problems	176
6.19	Is the change experiencing scope creep?	177
6.20	How paranoid is the Change Team about issues and problems?	179
6.21	Are staff comfortable raising issues and/or problems without the threat of repercussions from management or other colleges?	181
6.22	Is the Change Team being appreciated for their work and efforts?	184
6.23	Remember to keep checking whether the triggers, business case, benefits, etc. are still valid?	185
7	**Has sufficient preparation been performed for the go-live transition?**	**187**
7.1	Introduction	187
7.2	Has everything been delivered that is needed for transition? (And what are the impacts of any gaps)	188
7.3	Is everything that needs to be transitioned into live working as planned?	191
7.4	Has a Transition Coordinator been nominated?	194

7.5	Has the transition approach been agreed upon?	196
7.6	Is everybody aware that the transition is going to take place?	199
7.7	Is there clear ownership of the change before it is transitioned into live?	201
7.8	Has sufficient training been performed before go-live?	202
7.9	Is there a robust transition plan in place?	204
7.10	Is there a sufficient rollback plan in place?	207
7.11	Have both the transition and rollback plans been tested (both separately and together)?	209
7.12	Is the Change Team being appreciated for their work and efforts?	211

8 Care is still required during the actual transition event — 214

8.1	Introduction	214
8.2	Issues and problems will happen so prepare for them and a cool head is needed to manage them	215
8.3	Follow the pre-agreed transition and rollbacks plan and only diverge from them with extreme caution	217
8.4	Do not skip the control points within the transitions and roll-back plans	219
8.5	Do not forget the point of no return	222
8.6	Is the Change Team being appreciated for their work and efforts?	224

9 Remember that all changes need a certain amount of post-implementation support — 226

9.1	Introduction	226

9.2	Are all stakeholders aware that change takes time to bed in and this will mean the Change Team needs to be kept in place (often at a cost)	227
9.3	Is there are a clear set of handover criteria to pass the ownership of change from the Change Team to the required business teams?	229
9.4	Is the Change Team being appreciated for their work and efforts?	231

10	**There is still work to do even though the change is complete**	**233**
10.1	Introduction	233
10.2	Was the change been successful or not?	234
10.3	Has a post-implementation review of the lessons learnt exercise been completed?	236
10.4	Have all the successes been celebrated?	240
10.5	Has the change been formally closed?	242

11	**Conclusion and closing points**	**245**

Acknowledgements

The author would like to thank the following for their help in producing this book:

Chris Day (and everybody else at Filament Publishing) for their help, support and patience

Ana O'Sullivan and Jim Livesey for their thorough, honest and tactful review and feedback.

Margaret, Jessica, Molly, Tom and Elvis for just being there.

1 Introduction

Change is now key for the normal running of organisations. This is evidenced by phrases such as "change as usual".

Organisations need to change themselves to keep up with the constant change in their external environment. For example, new client demands, new/enhanced products, new regulations, keeping up with new technology advances etc. Therefore, it is important that organisations can implement change successfully otherwise they will struggle to operate and even potentially fail.

This means organisations need to develop a capability and the ability to implement change successfully. This capability covers many areas such as skilled staff, a supportive culture, suitable processes, suitable controls, etc. This capability can be viewed in a similar way to all the other capabilities an organisation needs to operate and succeed. For example selling, manufacturing, financing, marketing, etc.

However, despite the importance of implementing change successfully and an entire industry in place around to support change (such as consultancy, methodologies, training courses, professional qualifications, books, etc.) the record of implementing change is poor.

While there are no specific or reliable statistics in place, it is fair to say that few change initiatives are completely successful. There is always some type of issue or gap. For example, delayed implementation dates, requirements being missed, cost overruns, etc.

This book has been written to help organisations to improve their record of change.

It is not trying to present a 'silver bullet' approach or an 'off the shelf' model that all organisations can use to magically allow them to implement change perfectly. To be honest, this is impossible due to the complex nature of change and organisations generally

However, it does present a list of questions (grouped into seven themes) that organisations can ask themselves to ensure that they are implementing change successfully. Each question also contains a list of mitigations, hints-and-tips, suggestions, etc. to address any problems raised by asking the question.

These questions can be asked at various points during a change invitation. For example, they can be asked at the start of the change to ensure that the change starts in the best manner. They can be asked during the change project to allow organisations to review 'inflight' changes to check for problems. Finally, they can be asked at the end of a change to review how successful the change was, were the benefits for the change met and, if not, what were the causes of any problems so they can be addressed for both the change in questions plus any future changes.

The book itself contains 11 chapters plus a single Appendix

This first chapter is a short introduction.

Chapter Two provides a summary of the key definitions around change. For example, what is change? What is a project? What is a portfolio? Etc. While this is not critical to implementing change successfully, these definitions are used constantly but inconsistently. This creates confusion and misunderstanding. Therefore, for sanity, it is worthwhile having an agreed set of base-lined definitions.

Chapter Three provides a high-level summary of the seven key themes that are covered in the main part of this book.

This third chapter then leads into chapters 4 to 10 which cover each of these seven main themes.

The final chapter 11 provides a conclusion and wrap up of the key points.

Finally, there is an Appendix that provides a summary checklist of the key points and takeaways raised.

2 Definitions

2.1 Introduction

Before diving into the detail of how to make Change more successful, it Is worthwhile quickly stepping back and looking at three key definitions to ensure that they are fully understood; namely:

- What is change?

- What is a Project, Programme or Portfolio?

- What is Change Management?

These definitions are often used when implementing Change and it is key that they are all understood and used correctly.

2.2 What is change?

Defining the definition of change is much harder than it sounds. If one was to search the internet or academic journals, then one would find a large number of different definitions ranging from some very simple definitions to very long wordy definitions that are almost impossible to understand let alone to follow.

There are two main points of view when trying to define what change is.

From one point of view, some organisations and individuals look at change as an organic activity that happens naturally to organisations and the wider environment with no proactive effort to change or alter anything. For example, an organisation could offer two different products which initially had a revenue split of 50/50. However, the organisation's client base could change over time and this split could naturally or organically move (without any proactive effort by the organisation) to a 70/30 split.

However, secondly, common thinking these days across both professionals and academics, is that change is a proactive process where an organisation proactively define what they would be changing and then forms a 'ring fenced' piece of work to implement this change. For example, deciding to alter a part of the organisational structure to provide some sort of benefit to their stakeholders (such as trying to meet an organisation's strategy and/or version) and then creating a segregated piece of work to implement this change.

Therefore, for this book change is going to be defined as a

"Pre-emptive or pro-active modification to an organisation's activity and/ or its structure to provide some benefit to its stakeholders (such as staff, customers, regulators, the local community and shareholders)"

These activities to implement this proactive change are grouped into something called either a programme, portfolio or project. These three terms are defined in the next section.

2.3 What is a programme, a project, a portfolio or a change?

Similar to the definition of "change"(covered in section 2.2 above) these three terms are often mentioned and used both interchangeably and frequently. Again, if one was to search the internet or review professional or academic literature then one would find many differing and confusing definitions for them,

Therefore to provide some sort of clarity and consistency for this book, they will be defined as follows.

- **Project** – A project is designed to implement a single defined piece of organisational change to meet a business need or benefit.

    It will require a ring-fenced piece of work with associated money, resources, processes, etc. allocated to allow the project to be implemented. For example, a project to open a new office in a new location to increases sales will require the relevant people, the required money, etc. to be allocated to allow it to happen.

    Because of its singular nature, this means it is much easier to define and much easier to measure whether it is successful or not. For example, has the office been opened or not?

- **Programme** - A programme is a group of Projects gathered together to deliver a wider and usually more beneficial change within an organisation.

    Similar to the definition of a "project" above, a programme will require several different underlying ring-fenced pieces of work (again with sufficient budget (or capital), resources, processes, etc. in place), but it will also require an overarching governance 'umbrella' to control all the underlying pieces of work to ensure they are co-ordinated and implemented successfully.

    A programme could take any shape or size and it could last many years and contain many different overlapping and/ or sequential phases. For example, a programme could be formed to reduce day-to-day costs for an organisation. This means it could include several underlying projects covering outsourcing the data centre to cloud technology, offshoring operations development to low-cost regions, reducing staffing levels, cutting expenses, etc. which could be spread and/or phased over many years.

This wider nature means the scope can be harder to define which, in turn, means it can be more challenging to measure whether the programme holistically was successful or not. For example how successful would a programme be if only some of the underlying projects or changes were completed to reduce costs but others did not complete fully or were complete failures?

Also, it is not uncommon for unconnected projects to be included in a programme for ease of running.

- **Portfolio** – A portfolio is a set of projects and programmes that supports an organization's overall strategy for typically a pre-agreed period (such as a calendar year, financial year or for a future growth period).

    Again similar to the definitions of "project" and "programme" above, a portfolio will require several dedicated or ring-fenced pieces of work to be implemented. Each of these individual elements will require its budget, resources, processes, etc. There will also be an overarching governance structure to ensure all the elements of the portfolio are delivered. Because of the organisational-wide nature of portfolios then this governance structure could be very senior such as either a senior management committee or even a Board of Directors.

    For example, an organisation may have a strategy to increase profitability by 10% which means they will have a portfolio of projects and programmes to (a) try and met this strategic objective by say increasing revenue and reducing cost but (b) also to ensure the normal 'business-as-usual' changes are catered for such as ensuring the organisation is compliant with any regulation changes or ensuring they reduce their carbon footprints etc.

This means the scope of a Portfolio can be very wide although its success can be easier to measure because it matches the organisation's objectives. Using the example above, if the profitability is increased by 10% then it is possible to say the portfolio was successful at a high level.

The relationships between these three are summarized in the diagram below.

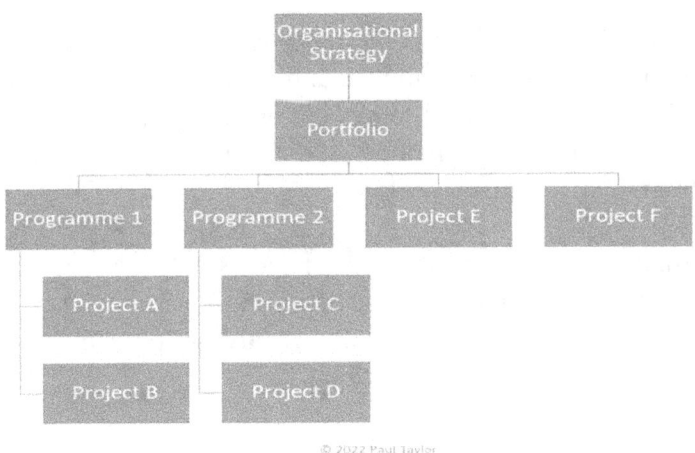

There is also a further term used which is called "Change". This is a much broader definition and it can cover any pro-active alternation to an organisation's operation or structure. Therefore it can cover minor changes that business teams will perform without any formal processes (such as updating operational checklists as part of normal continuous improvement). It also is used to cover the more formal projects, portfolios and programmes initiatives.

2.4 For clarity and ease of reading, this book will use the term "Change" to cover Projects, Programmes and Portfolios.

For ease of reading and to avoid confusion then this book will use the phrase "Change" to cover projects, portfolios and programmes. This is for three main reasons.

- Firstly it will make the book easier to read. If the phrases Project, Programme and Portfolio are constantly used and repeated then it will make the book very wordy and therefore very hard to follow.

- Secondly, the disciplines, approaches, hints-and-tips, etc. used across Projects, Programmes and Portfolios are very similar albeit at different levels of scale. For example, they all require supportive management, a good governance structure, good human management skills, etc.

- Finally, many organisations will have a single or set of changes team in place that will look after implementing all types of changes across an organisation regardless of whether it is a project, programme or portfolio.

2.5 What is change Management?

Now that this book has defined what a "Change" is and the differences and overlaps between Projects, Programmes and Portfolios, then the final key definition of "Change Management" needs to be agreed upon.

Again, this is another phrase that is often banded around with multiple definitions which can be over-complex, hard to understand and confusing.

However, "change management" is quite simply ensuring that there are suitable structures, controls, challenges, people, skills, capabilities, oversight, etc. in place to assure that any Change (i.e. Project, Portfolio or Programme) is implemented successfully. This will cover (a) defining clearly at the start what the Change is (b) implementing the change as effectively as possible (c) transitioning the change into the live environment as smoothly as possible (d) ensuring the change is supported and 'bedded in' appropriately and then finally (e) ensuring the Change is closed down.

3 The reasons for change failure

3.1 Introduction

The previous section (section 2) outlined some key definitions that are important when trying to implement change successfully.

This third section provides a high-level introduction or overview of the areas that organisations need to focus on and improve to increase the probability of implementing change successfully. In effect, it provides an overview of the rest of the book.

3.2 What are the seven factors that help and/or hinder change within organisations?

It is important to remember that Change is a complex activity with many interdependent factors and variables. For example, a lack of focus, poor controls, incorrect organisation structures, poor behaviours, inappropriate cultures, not having the ability to manage ambiguity, etc. A failure in one or more of these areas will greatly reduce the likelihood that a change will succeed. Therefore implementing change is a holistic activity.

To try and put some sort of structure around this 'madness' then these factors have been grouped into seven areas. Please see the diagram below.

A summary of each of these seven areas is provided below (but more detail is covered in Sections 4 and 10).

1 – Is the organisation capable of making the change?

The first element is whether an organisation is capable of making a change?

A large amount of professional and academic change literature focuses on what needs to be undertaken to successfully implement the Change is itself. For example, understanding its scope, understanding its success criteria, performing planning, problem management, issue management etc.

However, a substantial number of Change failures are linked to the organisation itself. For example, does the organisation have the right skills, people, structures, cultures and capabilities to implement a change successfully? Similarly, do organisations fully understand their customer base, their product base and the complexity of their operating models (especially if they contain internal suppliers, external suppliers, multiple locations and different time zones)? Finally, do organisations have any issues in their configuration that could cause issues such as internal silos, poorly skilled senior management, lack of controls, internal politics, etc.?

If any of these issues are in place then, regardless of how well a specific change is run, then the organisation will struggle to implement change successfully. This means they need to be addressed as soon as possible.

This area is discussed in much more depth in Section 4.

2 – Has enough preparation work been performed??

The second factor relates to whether the organisation implementing the Change performed sufficient preparation work for the Change?

The old saying of "perfect planning prevents poor performance" is so very true for Change Management. It is not uncommon for organisations to jump into making a Change without doing any pre-work or planning. For example not understanding the strategic reason for the change, not understanding what the success criteria is, not ensuring all stakeholders are brought into the change etc. It is unclear why this happens to be honest but it may be a case of people seeing a problem and then wanting to fix it immediately without stepping back and thinking in detail about 'what really needs to be done'

A lack of upfront thought and pre-planning is a key reason for failure.

This is discussed in Section 5

3 – Is the change being implemented in the best method?

The third item element relates to whether the change is being implemented in the best method?

There is almost a limitless number of ways that a Change could be implemented but the most appropriate method must be selected for the Change in question. For example are there suitable senior management involved in overseeing the change? Are people working long hours? Are there suitable governance controls in place? How supportive and knowledgeable is the management? How are the Change Team managing internal and external suppliers plus many others? How well is progress being tracked? Are staff comfortable raising issues and/or problems without the threat of repercussions from management or other colleges? Etc.

Implementing a change inappropriately is another key reason for change failure.

This is discussed in section 6 in more depth.

4 – Has there been sufficient preparation for the 'transition into live' event?

The fourth element relates to has the organisation in question prepared sufficiently for the transition event or events?

All changes have some sort of go-live or transition event. This could be a single 'big bang' switch over such as upgrading a piece of technology or it could be a pre-planned phased approach such as rolling out a new product launch over several weeks or months. Therefore it is essential that sufficient planning, preparation and testing is performed before the transition event is attempted. For example, is there clear ownership of the change post-transition, has adequate training been performed, has the transition plan been tested, has any roll-back plans been tested, etc.

There is no point in spending a large amount of effort, stress, time, money, etc. on implementing a change if the Change Team fail to transition the change into the live environment smoothly. This means that pre-transition work is essential for this. Poor transition planning is another reason for change failure. This subject is discussed in more detail in section 7

5 – Has the change been transitioned smoothly and successfully into the live or production environment?

This fifth factor is a follow-up to the "pre-transition planning" item mentioned directly above.

Even if a significant amount of thorough pre-transition planning is completed then, without wanting to state the obvious, the transition itself must be executed as perfectly as possible. For example, ensuring the transition plan is followed, all required controls are in place, etc. Poor transition execution or implementation is another reason for change failure.

This area is discussed in more detail in section 8

6 – Is there sufficient post-transition support for the change?

This factor links directly from items 4 and 5 listed above.

Once the change is transitioned into production then the change is still not fully complete. All changes will need some type of post-transition support or 'bedding in'. (This work is sometimes called Warranty or Hypercare support). This could cover areas such as ensuring the Change Team is kept together to provide support to the new business owners, ensuring the change ownership is handed over to the business teams, ensuring the change teams are disbanded, etc.

The failure to manage post-implementation support is another reason for change failure. It would be a real shame if a change is transitioned smoothly but encountered problems because the post-implementation support was ineffective.

This area is debated in more detail in section 9.

7 – Has the change been closed down properly and fully?

The seventh and final element relates to the activities to close a change when it is completed.

Once a change is fully transitioned into production then it needs to be formally closed. This will allow the business owners to take ownership of the change and for the Change Team to be fully disbanded. If a change is not formally closed then they have a habit of running on forever.

Also as part of this closure, it would be essential to determine whether the change was successful (or not), and it would be a good idea to complete a lessons learnt review and celebrate any successes

The failure to fully close a change is another reason for failure.

This is explored in more detail in section 10.

4 Does the organisation have the skills and capabilities to implement Change successfully?

> *"An empowered organisation is one in which individuals have the knowledge, skill, desire, and opportunity to personally succeed in a way that leads to collective organisational success"*
> *- Stephen Covey*

4.1 Introduction

Change is now part of normal business operations and this can be evidenced with terms such as "change as usual"

However, most of the change literature and supporting training courses tend to focus on implementing a specific change itself. For example, understanding scope, understanding success criteria, planning, managing problems etc. However, a large number of changes failures are caused by the organisation implementing the change not having the capabilities to implement changes successfully.

Having the capabilities to implement a successful change is an organisational capability that needs to be in place (especially with the constant nature of change). This is along the same lines as the capability to market products, distribute products, manage finance, manage technology, etc. If a change capability does not exist then it needs to be developed pretty urgently.

This capability is discussed in more detail within this section but it can be split into three main areas.

1. The first area relates to issues or capabilities that are internal to the organisations and often not that visible to the outside world.

   For example, does the organisation have the right skills, people, structures, cultures and capabilities to implement a change successfully? If there are issues or problems in this area then, because these are internal issues, then an organisation should look to address them as soon as possible. If they are not addressed then they will cause challenges when trying to implement any change.

2. The second area relates to issues that are caused by the external environment that the organisation operates within.

   For example, does the organisation fully understand their customer base, their product base, the regulatory environment they operate in, etc.? Because these are external factors then an organisation may not have much power or scope to change them. However, they should be aware of them so they can implement contingencies and mitigations.

3. The final area relates to issues that cross the internal and external barriers of an organisation.

   This area relates primarily to the complexity of the operating model that underpins the day-to-day, monthly, annual, etc. running of an organisation. Nearly all organisations' operating models consist of a 'spaghetti' of attributes plugged together. For example different internal processes, different technology, different people, etc. as well various internal suppliers, external suppliers, multiple locations and different time zones.

   While it may be possible for an organisation to change certain internal parts of their operating model, they may struggle to change the external parts especially if these are being supplied by an external supplier or part of market infrastructure. Therefore it is important that an organisation fully understands all aspects of their operating model because any materials gaps in knowledge will result in problems with implementing changes which could result in failures.

The structure of this section is based on a list of questions grouped in the three sections listed above. Each question focuses on a particular problem that can hinder or help successful change.

INTERNAL ISSUES

4.2 Has the organisation grown by acquisition?

Firms that have grown by acquisition often struggle to implement change successfully.

This is because they are often silo'ed which results in a large amount of internal politics and protectionism between the employees of the merged and/or the acquired organisations. This causes real problems when implemented changes because it (a) restricts the teams working together effectively (b) stops the flow of information between different parts of the organisation and (c) generally creates tension and distrust across all areas.

Furthermore, when acquisitions are completed, operating models are often not combined effectively. This is mainly due to the cost, effort and general difficulty required to complete this. Once acquisitions are completed, organisations are often keen to look at the 'next big thing' as opposed to completing the acquisition fully by, for example, merging operations, combining cultures, merging or removing duplicate products, etc. This means post-acquisition operating models often consist of duplicate functions, duplicate products, duplicate services and a 'spaghetti' of duplicate processes. This confusion and complexity hinder making change successful.

The author once worked a change for an organisation that was the result of several mergers and acquisitions where none of the operating models, client base or product range had been merged. Therefore there was an amount of duplicated functions, products, client records and (in particular) technology. This meant that when a regulatory change was implemented then it was necessary to perform the same 'change' across the different duplicate parts of the operating model. This increased substantially costs, effort and complexity.

Unfortunately, organisations that have grown by acquisitions are part of organisational life and it is unlikely something that Change Teams can address on their own. However, it is important to identify any issues found because any associated complexity and increased costs and effort will need to be catered for in the change plan, budget and other change documents. It is also worthwhile ensuring the Steering Committee and Sponsor are aware of these problems so they can help if required

Key Takeaways

- Growth by acquisition is a part of organisational life and it is unlikely something that Change Team can address on their own,

- However, it is important to identify any issues here because any associated complexity will need to be catered for in the change plan, budget and other change elements.

- It is also worthwhile ensuring the Steering Committee and Sponsor are aware of these problems so they can help if required.

4.3 How much autonomy from the parent does the organisation have?

Firms that do not have much autonomy from their parents struggle to implement change successfully. This is due to a lack of freedom that causes slow decision making which in turn causes friction and a general environment of distrust, delay and just feeling constrained.

If this is noted then the Change Manager needs to raise this with the Sponsor and Steering Committee to ensure that they are aware of any problems that this could cause.

While this lack of autonomy is often an organisational-wide problem, there are some options that the Change Team could follow to reduce the impacts.

- The first option is to try and obtain more autonomy from the parent itself. But if this is not available already then this may be hard to obtain especially within the timelines. However this no harm is asking.

- The second option is to try and get some delegated pre-approvals to allow the Change Team to make certain decisions on their own without parental approval. For example, pre-approving go-live decisions if certain pre-agreed factors are met or having the ability to enter into certain supplier contracts if they comply with a pre-agreed set of criteria.

- The third option (which is a variation on the second option to be fair) is for the parent to delegate responsibility (with pre-approved criteria) for certain decisions to somebody senior within the organisation making the change. This could be the Sponsor, Steering Committee or other senior management. For example, a certain individual can approve supplier contracts but for this change only but they cannot approve any other supplier contracts.

- The final option is to include somebody from the parent organisation in the Change. For example, the Change Team may want to include a senior member of the parent organisation as part of the Steering Committee. If they are part of the change then they may be able to help make decisions quicker than having to constantly refer up and down to the parent.

Key Takeaways

- The lack of empowerment is another fact of business life that the Change Team will struggle to fix themselves.

- However, if it does happen then it will cause issues with implementing change successfully.

- If this is noted then the Change Manager needs to raise this with the Sponsor and Steering Committee to ensure that they are aware of any problems that this could cause.

- However, some options can be used to provide some sort of mitigation such as requesting more autonomy, asking for pre-approvals, involving staff from the parent organisation and delegated decision making.

4.4 How silo'ed is the organisation?

Firms that are silo'ed in nature struggle to implement change successfully.

While there are real benefits to having silos in an organisation. It allows certain parts of the workflow to be split up and/or be given to different specialist teams and organisations. This makes the process more effective and efficient. For example, within aerospace, the development of the wings and the engine can be given to specialist firms or teams who will perform the work separately and each part will be 'plugged' together at a later stage. Likewise, for call centres, different operations can be set up around the world to provide 24 hours per day coverage across every day of the year.

However, having silos can both restrict the flow of the data across the organisation and the ability for an organisation to work together effectively. This can make implementing change successfully more challenging.

Although there are some mitigating actions.

- The most obvious one would be to involve people from the different silos in the change so they can provide input and assistance. Although, for a large change spread across a large number of silos, this could be challenging.

- Any complexities around this will need to be included in the change plan, budget, issues, staffing etc.

- Finally, it would also be advantageous to ensure the Steering Committee and Sponsor are also aware of any challenges in this area and whether these are causing any problems to the change being implemented. In their senior roles, they may be able to provide some guidance and/or steer.

Key Takeaways

- Working with organisations with silos again is another factor of organisational life and it is something that the Change Team is very unlikely to address themselves.

- The best mitigation is to involve representation from each 'silo' within the Change Team. But for a large change spread across a large number of silos, this could be challenging.

- Regardless of any complexities around this will need to be included in the change plan, budget, issues, staffing etc.

- Finally, the Steering Committee and Sponsor must be also aware of any challenges in this area and whether these are causing any problems to the change being implemented.

4.5 How well is the Missions Statement and Strategic Direction understood?

All Organisations and firms should have a mission statement. The purpose of a mission statement is to provide some sort of steer and understanding regarding why the organisation exists. For example, what is a charity's charitable causes? What type of clients does a retailer serve? Does the organisation provide good customer service? Does the organisation offer cheaper fees than the competition? Etc. This means it is important that all stakeholders (covering internal staff, customers, suppliers, etc.) need to understand the Mission Statement.

Unfortunately, mission statements are met with a certain amount of scepticism with many individuals seeing them as pointless management speak and ignore them. Also, the understanding of the mission statement is often patchy. Some staff will understand the mission statement and will follow it religiously. Some staff may be aware of the mission statement but do not fully understand what it means and how it relates to their job. Some staff might be aware of the mission statement but do not believe it. Finally, there may be some people who may not even know that a mission statement exists.

There is clear evidence that if Change Team members understand the overall purpose of the organisation (i.e. the mission statement), then they could relate the change to this, which would in turn significantly improve the chances of success.

(Also, having an understanding of the mission statement, should hopefully ensure that changes not aligned to the mission statement are either stopped or enhanced so they do match the mission statement).

But if they do not understand it or there are gaps in the understanding then there are some mitigations that can be taken.

- At a holistic or pan-organisation level; once senior management becomes aware of any gaps in knowledge then they should re-communicate the mission statement via a communications outreach to all stakeholders. This outreach could be performed by face-to-face presentations, video conference presentations or via pre-recorded video messages. Any outreach should be backed up by training and presentations to staff if necessary.

- With the change itself, then the Sponsor, Steering Committee members or even the Change Manager should ensure all stakeholders impacted are aware of how the change fits in within the Mission Statement. For example, if the change in progress is to outsource manufacturing to a low-cost region and the Mission Statement says the organisation offers the cheapest products then the link between the two should be explained. Also, it is important to bear in mind that people will join and lead of Change Team over time. This means that it will be necessary to hold various 'refreshers' on this as people join the Change Team

Key Takeaways

- All Organisations and firms should have a mission statement.

- The purpose of a mission statement is to provide some sort of steer and understanding concerning why the organisation exists.

- All stakeholders (covering internal, suppliers, customers and others) should understand the mission statement of an organisation. If there are gaps in the knowledge then these need to be addressed immediately.

- All stakeholders involved in a change should understand how the change fits in with the Mission Statement.

- This clear understanding helps with implementing change successfully, and it will ensure that changes that do not match the missions statement are either stopped or enhanced to ensure it does match.

4.6 How well does the organisation react to Market and Industry changes?

At a general level, firms that react quickly to changes in the external market tend to be more successful. For example, they cope with new market movements such as exploiting social media and coping with using newer technologies (such as new manufacturing techniques, machine learning, Natural Language Processing, big data, etc.) better than firms who miss or do not understand these developments. Likewise, they also cope with new client needs such as self-service over mobile apps and websites. Finally, they also spot their competition making changes quicker so they can react by enhancing their products and services or even just copying the competition.

This ability to react to market movements quicker also allows change to be implemented more successfully. These firms will often see something that needs to change earlier than their competition, which means they can be on the front foot starting the change. In some cases, they may have finished the change before the competition has even started. This is a large competitive advantage.

At a change level, there is very little the Change Team can do to make an organisation react quicker to market and industry changes. This is because any poor behaviours are at an organisation-wide level. However, if the Change Manager does notice any issues then it would be advantageous to mention this to the Sponsor (both tactfully and on a one-to-one basis) because (a) they are accountable at a senior level and (b) they may be able to address this at their more senior level in the organisation by working with their management colleges.

Key Takeaways

- Organisations that react quicker and better to change in the market and industry will implement change more successfully

- However, if issues are noted in this area then there is very little the individual Change Team could do about this.

- Any problems should be escalated (both tactfully and on a one-to-one basis) to the Sponsor, senior management and Steering Committee members so they can take some holistic organisational-wide action

4.7 How much customer focus does the organisation have?

All firms and organisations say they have good customer service or their clients are at the centre of their organisations. (This can include both external and internal customers). But it is fair to say that many firms forget this in the heat of the battle when running an organisation. For example, for commercial organisations, there could be in house politics and infighting, which deflects the organisation away from giving good customer service. Likewise in a charity, there could be so much focus on running the charity which deflects effort away from ensuring that the beneficiaries of the charity are looked after

However, firms that have genuine customer focus tend to understand the marketplace much better. Firstly, this means they can grow and operate their businesses much better. Secondly, it means they are much more successful in implementing change because they understand the marketplace, the competition and customer needs. This means they can start changes earlier or understand the changes better which increases the chance of success greatly.

However, if issues are noted in this area then there is very little the individual Change Team could do about this. Any problems should be escalated (both tactfully and on a one-to-one basis) to the Sponsor, senior management and Steering Committee members so they can take some holistic organisational-wide action.

Key Takeaways

- Organisations that have a real customer focus (for both external and internal customers) will implement change more successfully

- However, if issues are noted in this area then there is very little the individual Change Team could do about this.

- Any problems should be escalated (both tactfully and on a one-to-one basis) to the Sponsor, senior management and Steering Committee members so they can take some holistic organisational-wide action

4.8 How well does the organisation learn from their mistakes?

All organisations say they learn from mistakes. One will struggle to find an organisation that would say publicly the opposite. However, despite all these bold statements and commitments, there is a long list of firms that appear to make the same mistake over and over again. For example, failures within changes (especially technology for some reason), poor products, poor customer services, poor supplier selection, naive planning, poor financial management plus many others

Some organisations will perform 'lessons learnt' studies or some type of post mortem review when problems do happen. However, these studies are very problematic. Firstly many organisations do not complete them for various reasons such as they are so relieved that the change is complete that they want to move on to the next change or they are nervous about what could be found and reported. Secondly, any findings and recommendations discovered (especially if uncomfortable) are sometimes ignored, hidden, disputed or not implemented.

However, there is clear evidence that organisations that genuinely learn from their mistakes both run their businesses better and also implement change more successfully.

If there does not appear to be a culture of learning lessons then this is a reflection of the organisation's culture. Any problems should be escalated (both tactfully and on a one-to-one basis) to the Sponsor, senior management and Steering Committee members because (a) they are accountable and (b) so they can take some organisational-wide action to address them.

Having said this, some suggestions can be followed at the individual change Level.

- Firstly, the Change Managers should ask for copies of any post mortems and post-implementation reviews of any similar changes implemented in the organisation previously. They can then study this documentation to understand what issues were encountered

- Secondly, Change Managers may be able to speak to people in the organisation about problems and issues on previous changes. It would be good if this was done on a 1-2-1 basis because it allows people to be more open and host, and therefore will provide some useful insights.

- Thirdly, and this is slightly more challenging, it may be possible to speak to suppliers, customers, industry participants regarding their previous changes implemented in the organisation. Again if this is done on a 1-2-1 basis then people will be more comfortable in being open and providing some insightful insights.

- Finally, the Change Manager may want to tactically speak to the Sponsor and other senior management about any previous issues that have been encountered. Because these people are senior then they may be able to provide some useful suggestions and insights.

The result is that the Change Manager should gather a 'bucket load' of useful insights which can be incorporated into the change going forward (such as updating plans, including more tasks, tracking certain parts of the change in more detail, etc.). This should improve the change's likelihood of success. Also, it would be advantageous to escalate (both tactfully and on a one-to-one basis) any larger problems discovered to the Sponsor, senior management and Steering Committee members

Key Takeaways

- All organisations say they learnt from their mistakes but there is clear evidence that organisations do not always do this.

- Organisations that do learn from their mistakes both (a) run their organisations much better and (b) implement change successfully.

- If the Change Manager and Change Team are worried about mistakes being repeated then two routes can be followed.

- Firstly they can gather data on previous 'errors' which help define the change going forward. This data can be obtained via previous change post mortems and tactfully speaking to people.

- Secondly, it would be advantageous to escalate (both tactfully and on a one-to-one basis) any larger problems discovered to the Sponsor, senior management and Steering Committee members

4.9 How much empowerment do staff have to make decisions?

Organisations that give staff empowerment to make decisions and to do their job without unreasonable controls tend to be run much more effectively. These organisations also tend to implement change more successfully.

However, it is noted that there is an awkward tipping point that needs to be managed here. At one end of the scale, an organisation needs to give its staff space to do their job otherwise they will feel constrained and held back which will result in general frustration, problems and staff leaving. At the other end of the scale, organisations cannot give their staff free access to do whatever they want because there would be no controls and they could make unchecked decisions which would result in issues and even complete chaos.

If the Change Manager believes that is not sufficient empowerment given to the staff within his change then several options can be explored:

- One option is to work with the Sponsor and other senior management on determining whether any further empowerment can be delegated to Change Team members. For example, do new roles and responsibilities need to be defined? What decisions people can make subject to pre-agree criteria? Etc.

- If this is not possible, then the Sponsor needs to be made aware of the problem that this lack of empowerment can cause. For example, delays in decision making could have a knock-on effect on deliverables. The Change Manager should ensure that these extra delays are covered by contingencies in the change such as by adding extra time in plans and money in the budgets

Key Takeaways

- Organisations that give staff empowerment to make decisions and to do their job without unreasonable controls tend to be run much more effectively (including implementing change more successful).

- If there is insufficient empowerment then may be possible (with the agreement of the Sponsor and other senior management) to temporarily allow more empowerment within the change.

- Regardless the Sponsor will need to be fully aware of any issues regarding this and what problems they cause with the change.

4.10 How supportive and knowledgeable are senior management?

At a general level, all organisations need senior skilled management to operate. These skills cover areas such as technical skills, soft skills and general management skills. If organisations do not have properly skilled management at the top, then they will either struggle or even eventually fail.

The same concept relates to change management but the required skill sets can be looked at in three slightly different groupings.

- The first area is ensuring that senior management is skilled in the technical area of change. For example, if the change relates to aerospace and the management understand aerospace, if the change relates to manufacturing then the management is skilled in manufacturing etc. If they have a good understanding of this area, then they can challenge and raise issues as well as provide general support if required.

- The second area is having skills in change management as a discipline. For example understanding planning, understanding risk management, understanding supplier management etc. Again if they have a good understanding of this area, then they can challenge and raise issues as well as provide general support if required.

- The third area is that senior management needs to be supportive of the change. Successful change is assisted where there is clear, constant and consistent support for the change from management.

However, if there are some skill gaps then there are a few options

- At an organisational general level, there is very little that the change can do to address this apart from maybe having a very tactful and probably awkward conversation with a Sponsor to raise this with them so they can raise this with their management peers.

- At the change level, there are a few things that can be done but again, they are challenging and could be awkward for the Change Manager.

Firstly, the Change Manager or the Change Team generally will need to spend more time with senior management as a group to talk them through problems and explain issues. This could be a drag on their time.

It would also be advantageous for the Change Manager to spend more time on a 1-2-1 basis with various senior managers to explain any specific issues that relate to their area and allow them to ask in-depth questions that they may feel awkward about asking in front of the wider management group. This 1-2-1 interactive will also build trust and rapport which will, in turn, improve the working relationship between the Change Manager and senior management.

A side effect of this is if senior management does not understand all the issues, then they could unreasonably blame the Change Manager or the Change Team for problems that are not their fault. Some organisations operate around this employing short term experts in the technical area being changed and/or within change management generally. This provides general support for the Change Manager and also provides some sort of comfort for the senior management additionally.

Key Takeaways

- Without suitably skilled senior management support then a change will almost indefinitely fail.

- One could argue there is no point starting at change unless senior management are suitably skilled

- However, if there are gaps then there is very little the Change Team can do at the organisation-wide level apart from tactfully ensuring the Sponsor and Steering Committee are aware.

- But there are some mitigating options at the individual change level which can be actions For example spending more time with senior management, explaining issues in more detail or looking to temporarily recruit experts.

4.11 How well does the organisation's culture manage the human aspects?

All organisations have some sort of culture. In effect is like the personality of an organisation. Some cultures are aggressive, others are passive, some are untrustworthy, some are very helpful etc.

Management theorists nowadays put a large amount of emphasis on changing an organization's culture to help the company improve itself. For example, make it more successful, help it deal with its clients better, help it react to issues quickly and also to help it implement change more successfully. (Many organisations have performed changes to proactively alter their culture to something they feel is better although it is unclear how successfully many of these are because of the gap between management and day-to-day running of the organisation as well as the difficulties of changing a culture).

An organisation's culture heavily influences whether an organisation is successful at a holistic level.

The culture is also heavily significant on whether a change is successful or not and in particular in how it manages the human aspects of a change. It is important to remember that change is effectively a social process. Change is triggered by people, implemented by people and the implemented change is ultimately used by people.

Most change theory tends to focus on the technical aspects of change such as managing scope, solution design, having technical knowledge etc. The human elements tend to be forgotten. For example conflict management, resistance management, coping with fear, addressing suspicion, managing scepticism, correctly rumours and challenging false news.

However, if the human factors are not managed successfully, then it will cause problems. These problems could fester into something quite nasty, such as major disagreements, arguments, and people generally falling out.

Therefore an organisation (and individual Change Teams) will need an appropriate and supportive culture that will ensure any human factor related issues are addressed and resolved as soon as possible. It is important to remember that Change Team members on the whole want to get involved in the change, be confident to express their ideas, feel motivated and feel proud to be part of the Change Team.

At the organisation level, it is very hard for an individual Change Manager to fix anything if there are major human factor issues. These issues are part of the wider organisation and senior management will need to address these. However it would be worthwhile for the Change Manager to tactfully express concerns to the Sponsor so they can work with senior management to address them.

But if there are issues at the change specific level, there are some mitigations that can be followed

- The first area is that the Change Manager needs to be paranoid about any human or cultural related issues that are happening or likely to happen. Therefore, the Change Manager needs to constantly monitor the team to see if they can spot any issues.

- It would also be worthwhile speaking tactfully with other areas outside the Change Team (such as other members of the organisation, customers and suppliers) to sense if have noticed any issues.

- If issues are found and need to be addressed immediately. It is very much along the lines of a 'stitch in time saves nine'. Remember that human-related issues can fester which means they will grow into something nasty and horrible that could permanently damage the change and be impossible to fix.

- The actions that can be taken depends on the circumstances and the people involved. For example,

The Change Manager (and if necessary the Sponsor) could work with the individuals involved to help them work together. In effect some sort of mediation

Also, the Change Manager (and, again, if necessary the Sponsor) could work with impacted people to ensure they are aware that their behaviour is upsetting others or causing problems and then work with them to change their behaviours.

Depending on the nature of the issue, it might be necessary to change the structure of the Change Team to work around the problems. For example, it may be necessary to move individuals to different parts of the team so they do not have to work with each other. Also, it may be necessary to change desk layouts so the 'fighting' team members do not have to sit with each other.

Finally, it may be necessary to remove people from the team completely if they are unwilling to change. This could cause immediate problems if a key person has to leave but sometimes in the longer term this is the best option.

Key Takeaways

- Any human factor related issues must be identified and addressed urgently otherwise they will grow into major issues which result in the change failing.

- Unfortunately, it is very challenging to manage human issues and most people, including Change Managers, will feel very uncomfortable about tackling them but it is, unfortunately, part of the job.

- At the organisation level, it is very hard for an individual Change Manager to fix anything if there are major human factor issues. These issues are part of the wider organisation and senior management will need to address these. However it would be worthwhile for the Change Manager to tactfully express concerns to the Sponsor so they can work with senior management to address them.

- However, some improvements could be made by the Change Manager to help smooth the change running.

4.12 Does the organisations have an organisation-wide committee to oversee all changes that are either planned or in progress?

Change is an ongoing activity within organisational life. Therefore this means that each organisation needs to have a solid and robust set of change processes to ensure that the implementation of any change is controlled which in turn will increase its chance of success.

One of the key parts of this is that every organisation needs to have a "Senior Organisation-wide Change Oversight Committee" that will oversee all changes progress across the organisation. Apart from tracking progress and issues, it will ensure the organisation deploys its limited change capacity on the most important changes and in the most effective way.

The structure of this Senior Organisation-wide Change Oversight Committee depends on the organisation in question. For example, it could be part of the wider senior management or executive group, or it could be a separate forum that reports to the senior or executive management group.

However, all Steering Committees (see section 5.15 above) for each Change in progress will need to report to this Senior Organisation-wide Change Oversight Committee.

Organisations without a Senior Organisation-wide Change Oversight Committee will struggle to implement change successfully. This is because they will not formally track progress at a senior level, issues will be missed and the organisation will not use its resources most effectively.

The specific responsibilities for this Senior Organisation-wide Change Oversight Committee are as follows:

- Approving that a new change can start

- Ensuring change is planned holistically across all changes in progress. Especially if there are dependencies between different changes. For some organisations, there could be hundreds of changes in progress.

- Tracking the progress of change in execution and providing any error or challenge in the event of problems.

- Approving that a change can be paused or stopped if required.

- Approving that a change is completed and can formally close.

- Ensuring all material risks, issues and problems across all the Changes in progress are tracked and managed as required.

- Ensuring the organisational-wide change resources are managed effectively, namely:

  - This will cover the scope of physical resources such as desks floor space and technology

  - It will also ensure there are sufficient people with suitable skills and experience to manage the list of changes in progress. This can cover (a) hard skills such as planning, risk management, etc. (b) soft skills such as stakeholder management, and dealing with difficult people and (c) the various technical skills that relate to the organisation such as manufacturing or engineering.

  - It is also important as part of this, that the organisation ensure there are no single person dependencies. If any are identified then they need removing

- Reviewing Post Implementation Reviews from earlier changes to see what recommendations are appropriate and should be implemented organisation-wide.

Key Takeaways

- All organisations must have some type of change management processes and procedures in place.

- As part of this, every organisation must have a "Senior Organisation-wide Change Oversight Committee" that will oversee all changes progress across the organisation.

- This committee will track progress and issues as well as ensure the organisation deploys its limited change capacity on the most important changes and in the most effective way.

- Organisations without a Senior Organisation-wide Change Oversight Committee will struggle to implement change successfully. This is because they will not formally track progress at a senior level, issues will be missed and the organisation will not use its resources most effectively.

4.13 Does the organisations have an organisation-wide Change Management process that can be used for all Changes that need to be made?

As noted earlier, Change is an ongoing activity within organisational life. Therefore this means that each organisation needs to have a solid and robust set of change processes to ensure that the implementation of any change is controlled which in turn will increase its chance of success.

Another key part of this is to ensure that each organisation has a clear and understood Change management process in place that each Change in progress can follow. Without this in place then Change Managers may not have the tools to run changes and also there will not be consistency across changes are made. The result is confusion with an increased probability of change failure.

Although in reality, this standard change process should act as a baseline and specific changes should be able to tailor elements of it to meet the nature of the change being implemented. For example, moving manufacturing to a low-cost region will require a very different approach and set of documents than say running a change to improve the customer service.

It will need to contain the following elements:

- How to initiate a change,

- How to plan a change,

- How to report progress,

- How to run a working group meeting

- How to run a Steering Committee meeting

- What documents and artefacts need to be completed during the execution of a change? For example, planning documents, design documents, approvals documents, testing documents etc.

- How to close a change

- How to complete post-implementation reviews (including attestations and lessons learnt)

- How to document and manage risks, issues and problems.

- A selection of change templates. For example plans, initiation documents, progress reports etc.).

- How should documents be stored in document repositories? And what are the rules for deleting, amending, accessing, auditing and distributing these documents?

- A selection of best practices and 'things to look out for'

It is also important to remember that customers, suppliers, regulatory and industry bodies will have their change processes and the organisation may need to integrate into these processes as well.

Key Takeaways

- All organisations must have some type of change management processes and procedures in place.

- Another part of this is that a clear and understood Change management process is in place that each Change in progress can follow.

- Without this, the Change Managers may not have the tools to run changes and also there will not be consistency across changes are made. The result is confusion with an increased probability of change failure

4.14 Does the organisations have an organisation-wide Change Control process to manage changes in scope, timelines, etc. for inflight changes?

As noted above in section 4.13, each organisation needs an organisational-wide process to manage change.

Linked to this there should also be a set of processes to manage alterations to the change itself. Despite the best of efforts, changes will encounter issues that will require an alteration to it. For example, changing delivery dates, requesting more money, removing items from scope, etc.

This means there should also be an organisational-wide Change Control Policy and set of processes to review any changes to scope, timeline and costs on an in-flight change. The purpose of this is to ensure all alterations are assessed, reviewed and approved (or rejected) by the required management forums. Without this in place then alterations will be made 'on the fly' which will result in (a) individual changes either having issues or even failing (b) the organisation not managing all the individual changes in progress effectively and (c) a generally not knowing what is happening.

The actual process can be structured as follows:

1. A Change Request is raised. This will typically be performed by the Change Manager (with support from the Change Team) and approved by the Change Sponsor.

2. The Change Request is then impact assessed. This will need to be performed by the Change Team, subject-matter-experts and other key people (such as Finance, Technology, Engineering, Legal, etc.).

3. The Change Request will be reviewed and approved/rejected by the required stakeholders. For smaller or lower impact Change Requests then they may only need to be approved by the Sponsor or the Steering Committee. However for larger Change Requests then they may need to be approved by the "Senior Organisation-wide Change Oversight Committee" (mentioned in section 4.12 above) or even by more senior forums such as Executive Groups or even the Boards of Directors.

If the change is rejected then either (a) the Change Request cannot happen and is dropped or (b) the Change Request may require more refinement (such as further impact assessment or investigating other options) and then will need to be re-submitted.

4. Finally, once the change is approved then it needs to be communicated to all stakeholders, formally logged in the change documentation and then actually implemented.

Key Takeaways

- All organisations must have some type of change management processes and procedures in place.

- This means there should also be an organisational-wide Change Control Process to review any changes to scope, timeline and costs on an in-flight change.

- The purpose of this is to ensure all alterations are assessed, reviewed and approved (or rejected) by the required management forums.

- Without this in place then alterations will be made 'on the fly' which will (a) result in individual changes either having issues or even failing and (b) result in the organisation not managing all the individual changes in progress effectively.

4.15 Are the various Change Management processes a good 'cultural' fit for the organisation?

While sections 4.12 to 4.14 above discuss the critical importance of having oversight, controls, etc. in place to increase the probability of change success, these must match the culture and the context of the organisation.

For a small nimble organisation, having a complex overbearing change process will choke it and cause problems. Likewise, for a large organisation having a very light process will probably mean issues are missed, which will also cause problems.

Therefore, a poor culture or context fit could result in change problems and possibly even failure.

Key Takeaways

- As noted several times earlier all organisations must have some type of change management processes and procedures in place.

- However, these must match the culture and the context of the organisation

- A poor cultural or context fit could result in change problems and possibly even failure.

4.16 What should an organisation do if they do not have any or insufficient Change Management processes?

As discussed in sections 4.12 to 4.15 above, having sufficient oversight, controls, etc. is essential to aid the implementation of change successfully.

But what can an organisation do if either they do have this place or what they have in place is not fit-for-purpose?

Fortunately, there are some hints and tips at an organisational level:

- First of all, it is possible to buy processes off the shelf from various management schools and/or consultants. The disadvantage of this is often expensive and the processes could be overkill and may not match the organisation's size and culture. However, on the positive side, these processes can be purchased and implemented reasonably quickly.

- The second option is to employ a set of consultants to help develop a change process. This still could be expensive and take some time to fully complete. However, once the process is completed then it should be a fit for the organisation's size and culture.

- Alternative the organization themselves can start to pull together change processes using its staff and their experiences. This approach often acts as a good starting point but it is important to bear in mind this initial process may need to evolve as the organisation experiences more change

There are also some hints and tips at the individual change level. If no processes exist then it will be necessary to create a process specifically for the change in question. The Change Manager, Sponsor and Change Team should work together to create one. It could be based on previous experiences and from taking inputs from other areas such as Post Implementation Reviews and Lessons Learnt documents.

The advantage is that the processes design will be a good fit for change and possibly the organisation. This means it could be the basis for an organisational change process. However, the disadvantage is a major deflection in time and effort that should spend on actually implementing the change.

Key Takeaways

- As mentioned several times earlier (especially in sections 4.12 to 4.15), all organisations must have some type of change management processes and procedures in place.

- If it is not in place, then one needs to be implemented whether at an organisation level or something specific is created just for the change in question.

4.17 How susceptible is the organisation to the latest management and/or change 'fads'?

All industries are continuously developing a large number of new ways of working (a) to improve the way the industry and its organisations operate which should then (b) provide benefits to their customers, stakeholders and maybe even society as a whole.

These new ways of working are often developed by consultants, academia, organizations, etc.

At a general level, some examples are listed below:

- 360-degree feedback

- Business process re-engineering

- Offshore, nearshoring, right sourcing, etc.

- Outsourcing, near-sourcing, right-sourcing, etc.

- Flat organisations

- Hierarchical organisations

- Matrix Management

- Management by consensus

- Management by wandering around

- Open-plan offices

- Working from home

- Knowledge organisations

- Cloud computing

- Artificial intelligence

- Plus many others.

There is also a large number of specific new ways of working that have been developed to help implement change successfully. For example, lean management, agile management, sprints, waterfall, iterative management, etc. Again these have been developed by a combination of consultants, trade bodies, academia and other organisations

While all of these have real benefits to organisations and can help them to improve, it is important that before adopting them that the organizations fully understand what they offer, how they can help? How they can be implemented? What do they cost? What their disadvantages are? Etc.

This will allow organisations to take a sober view to see if these new ways of working can provide real benefits before they spend a vast amount of money or even look to adopt them. Otherwise, organisations will be perceived as trying to follow the latest trend or fad without any real benefit. This creates a large amount of uncertainty, scepticism from staff, waste money, waste time and a general distraction from everything else that the organisation is trying to do.

This also impacts a firm's ability to implement change successfully.

Key Takeaways

- The latest management new ways of working can provide real benefits to organisations and their stakeholders.

- However, it is important to ensure that organisations understand the benefits before they are implemented.

- Otherwise, it will cause problems with the organisations and impact its ability to implement change successfully

EXTERNAL ISSUES

4.18 How regulated is the environment that the organisation operates in?

All regulation is complex. Ask anyone who has worked in health, aerospace, construction or Financial Services recently and they will be willing to attest to this statement

Unfortunately, implementing change within a heavily regulated environment is challenging for four reasons.

- Firstly, all regulation is hard to understand, which means it is hard to implement changes to ensure an organisation complies with them.

- Secondly, many organisations will do the bare minimum amount of work to implement regulations. While all organisations see regulations as important, they also see it as using resources, money, effort, etc. which could be used much better elsewhere implementing new products or reducing costs. Therefore organisations will limit the amount of effort on regulation which means the change will have limited access to people, money and other resources. This means implementing change successfully is harder.

- Thirdly, it is important to note that other changes may require regulatory approval to be implemented which can be a time-consuming process. For example, if the Change Team is launching a new financial product then it will need approval from the organisation's local regulator. This means the level of change complexity will increase because it will be more costly and slower to implement. There is also the risk the regular may not allow a change to be made or only allow it to be implemented with certain refinements.

- Fourthly, this situation is often made worse by organisations that work across many different jurisdictions because they are often exposed to different and sometimes contradictory regulations.

Therefore these factors, delays and extra work will need to be incorporated into any change plans. Also, all stakeholders (such as Sponsors and Steering Committee members) must be aware of the regulatory 'drag' with the change and the associated possible impacts. Firstly they need to be aware because it is their job and secondly, they may be able to provide guidance and steer how to manage the regulators and any issues or problems.

(In fact, it is not uncommon for changes or products to be cancelled or substantially re-through due to regulatory impacts. For example, in financial services, some firms stopped offering certain client products because of the increased regulatory overhead and associated costs. The ironic result is that this negatively impacted the clients by removing product offerings that the regulation was supposed to protect).

Key Takeaways

- To be honest, not much can be done about the amount of regulation in the industry. It is a fact of life working within those industries.

- However, when making changes, it is important to ensure that the change understands the regulatory impact because it could impact the likelihood of success. These impacts will need to be reflected in change plans, costs, activity, etc.

- All stakeholders (such as Sponsors and Steering Committee members) must be aware of the regulatory 'drag' with the change and the associated possible impacts.

4.19 How complex is the client base?

All organisations have clients at some level or another. For example, charities would have the people who benefit from their charitable cause, commercial organisations will have paying customers and governments will have their voters and other stakeholders that they represent.

All these different types of clients bring their own set of challenges. For example different product needs, different servicing requirements, different regulatory demands, different profit margins etc. For example, a telecommunications provider will offer a very different set of products and services to an individual retail client than they would to a large corporate or government client. Likewise, a construction firm working on a small domestic development will offer a much simpler service than if they were working on a large building complex

The complexity of the client base must be understood because if there are any client implications in a change that are missed or handled incorrectly then it could upset the clients and cause the organisation issues as well as hindering whether the change is implemented correctly. There are two options to follow if the complexity of the client base is not fully understood by the change:

- The first option is to fully document all the types of clients held. This is the best method and it should be reasonably simple to do although it could take some time to collate all the information. One would hope that the individual client teams fully understand their clients. If there are any unknowns then these need to be documented.

- The second option is to include representatives from the client-facing teams in the change. If there are any client impacts then they can be referred to for steer and guidance. Even if the complexity of the client base is understood then it is still a good idea to involve some from the client-facing teams in the change.

Any complexity caused by the client base (especially if there are any unknowns) will need to be included in the change plan and budgets. For example, it may be necessary to include extra tasks, add contingencies, include more up-front analysis etc.

It is also important to ensure that both the Sponsor and the Steering Committee are aware of any client complexities (especially if there are any unknowns). It will ensure that the Steering Committee is accountable for any problems and they may be able to provide some steer or guidance on addressing them.

Finally (as mentioned earlier) it would a good idea to include members of the client-facing teams in the change to ensure any client issues are managed effectively. They could be included in working groups or within the Steering Committee. Also, depending on the client impact or the type of clients (such as corporate or institutional) then it may be necessary to think about involving the clients directly in the change. It may be necessary to create a specific working group for clients or even have individual working groups for each client.

Key Takeaways

- All organisations have a complex set of clients. It is a fact of organisational life.

- It is important to understand the complexity of the client base otherwise it will make implementing successful change more challenging.

- If this complexity is not fully understood then further analysis is required although hopefully, it should be a reasonably simple piece of work.

- Any complexity (or gaps in knowledge) need to be factored in the change and the Steering Committee and other senior management need to be aware.

- Finally, depending on the client's impact by the change, then it may be worthwhile to involve clients (either directly or via internal client-facing teams) in the change.

4.20 How complex is the set of products and/or services offered?

All organisations offer a range of products and services. These can range from very simple products and services to complex products and services. For example, within financial services, organisations will offer very simple products for retail or individual investors but they will also offer far more complex and sophisticated products and services for larger clients such as pension plans, corporations or national government. The same can be said for technology providers and manufacturers.

All these different types of products and services bring their own set of challenges. For example, different client needs, different servicing requirements, different regulatory demands, different profit margins, different market assessments, etc. A training firm will offer a very different service to an individual or retail client than they would to a large corporate or government client.

The complexity of the product or service base must be understood because if there are any product or service implications in a change that are missed or handled incorrectly then it could upset clients and cause the organisation issues. It could also mean that the change is not implemented correctly. There are two options to follow if the complexity of the product and service base is not fully understood by the change:

- The first option is to fully document all the types of products and services offered. This is the best method and it should be reasonably simple to do although it could take some time to collate all the information. One would hope that the individual business teams fully understand what products and services an organisation offers. If there are any unknowns then these need to be documented.

- The second option is to include representatives from the product ownership teams in the change. If there are any product impacts then they can be referred to for steer and guidance. Even if the complexity of the product base is understood then it is still a good idea to involve some from the product owning teams in the change anyway.

Any complexity caused by the product and service base (especially if there are any unknowns) will need to be included in the change plan and budgets. For example, it may be necessary to include extra tasks, add contingencies, include more up-front analysis etc.

It is also important to ensure that both the Sponsor and the Steering Committee are aware of any client complexities (especially if there are any unknowns). The Steering Committee may be able to provide some steer or guidance.

Finally (as noted earlier) it would a good idea to include members of the product ownership teams in the change to ensure any product and service issues are managed effectively. They could be included in working groups or within the Steering Committee.

Key Takeaways

- All organisations have a complex set of products and services. It is a fact of organisational life. The bigger the organisation then the wider and more complex range of products and services that will be offered.

- It is important to understand the complexity of the product and service base otherwise it will make implementing successful change more challenging.

- If this complexity is not fully understood then further analysis is required although hopefully, it should be a reasonably simple piece of work.

- Any complexity (or gaps in knowledge) need to be factored in the change and the Steering Committee and other senior management need to be aware.

- Finally, depending on the client's impact by the change, then it may be worthwhile to involve individuals from the product and service ownership teams directly in the change.

HYBRID INTERNAL AND EXTERNAL ISSUES

4.21 How well is the operating model understood?

All firms use a complex operating model to support their business. These models cover all the functions that an organisation needs to perform to operate daily. For example sales, distribution, manufacturing, engineering, delivery, finance and administration.

These models consist of a network of different components plugged together in a variety of manners. These individual components can be spread across many different locations, many different organisations (such as suppliers) and many different time zones. For example:

- Technology – This area could consist of a host of components. For example, old technology, in-house technology, supplier-provided technology, cloud computing, etc.

- Suppliers - All organisations use a combination of different suppliers to provide parts of their operating model. The service provided could either be bespoke services that are unique to the customer-supplier relationship or be standard 'off the shelf' services. This area is often more complicated if there is more than one supplier involved.

- Other parts of the organisation – Some organisations may use other parts of their internal group to provide part of the operating model as well. For example, there could be central legal teams, central technology teams (such as for data centres), central marketing teams or central human resource management teams.

- Procedures and processes – Holding and linking all these different components together, there are a variety of different processes in place. These processes can be manual, automated, paper-based, spreadsheet-based, email-based, processes plus many others. This area can be particularly complex.

- Multiple locations – Operating models are often spread over many different locations. This could be in the same building but on different floors, in different buildings, in different countries and across different time zones.

- Clients – This is an often overlooked area because clients are a key part of an operating model. For certain clients, there could be automated integration such as using websites or dedicated technology interfaces. For other types of clients the connection may be much looser; such as using paper or telephone connections

- Regulators – Depending on the industry then there may be integration with regulators. This could cover real-time activity (such as trading) or regular updates on incidents (such as health and safety violations).

- Industry infrastructure –There also may be integration with central industry infrastructure. This is common within financial services where there is central infrastructure for passing orders and making payments. Also, many firms use job boards for advertising opportunities etc.

- People – This element is often the people which is another area that is often overlooked or forgotten about. People are needed to run and maintain the operating model. These people will have different skills, different roles and can be spread across different locations. There could also be single points of failure where there is a single person where an organisation is reliant on a single person to support a part of the operating model.

- Culture – This area is often mentioned and often misused in organisational literature. Culture is an amalgamation of mutual beliefs and values established by its leadership to determine 'how the organisation does things'. This is further reinforced by the actions and behaviours within the organisation. In effect, culture could be viewed as the personality of the organisations

It is safe to say that even for the simplest organisations, operating models are complex and challenging to fully understand.

However, having said all this, the complexity itself of the operating model is not what normally causes problems with implementing change. It is normally a lack of understanding of both the operating model and its complexity that cause issues. In other words, a partially understood low complex operating model is likely to cause more issues than a complex operating model which is clearly understood, fully documented, etc.

Therefore it is important to understand the operating model (or the impacted parts of it) when implementing change. Fortunately, several options can help:

- The first option is to fully document the operating model with all gaps understood. This is the best method, but it will be difficult to do and will take time. This means it may not be possible if resources are limited and/or the change has tight timescales.

- The second and more common option is to include subject matter experts (SMEs) in the Change Team who understand the operating model (or at least the parts that could change). Therefore when the change is running and they have questions on the operating model these SMEs can be referred to for steer and guidance.

Regardless it will be prudent to cover the following as well.

- The first thing the Change Team should ensure is that any issues around either the complexity of the operating model or gaps in knowledge should be reflected in the change plan and budget. For example, any tasks or costs should include contingency elements to reflect these 'unknowns'.

- It would also be prudent to ensure the Steering Committee and Sponsor are aware of any issues which may cause some problems with implementing the change. Apart from ensuring these people are notified, they may be able to provide some help or steer on how to address the gaps.

Key Takeaways

- Complex operating models are a fact of life, especially for certain businesses. It is not something that any Change Team is likely to fix in their timescales.

- However, the Change Team must understand the complexity of the operating model, especially those elements that are impacted by the change. For example, which components and integrations will be impacted by the change?

- If there are gaps in this knowledge then they must be addressed before the change starts, otherwise, it will cause problems.

- Also, senior management should be made aware of these issues with any associated implications.

4.22 It is important to ensure that consistent terminology is used across all stakeholders.

As one will have noticed, there are many different definitions and terms used within change management. Section 3 documented four different terms for a change activity (namely a programme, a portfolio, a project and a change) and, for clarity, this book decided to use the term "change" to cover all types of change activities. Also, as one will notice when one reads other parts of this book, there are various other terms and phrases used. For example, Sponsor, Change Manager, Steering Committee, Project Board, Dry Run, Dress rehearsal plus many others.

Also, each industry will have its own set of terms and definitions in place. These can be complex, confusing and sometimes contradictory. For example, Financial Services, Education, Technology and Government all have a wide range of different and confusing terms which are challenging to understand, even to those who have worked there for many years.

Therefore, to avoid any confusion and unnecessary problems, then it is important to agree on a consistent set of terms and definitions for all stakeholders (such as internal parties, external suppliers, customers, regulators, etc.) covering both Change Management and the industry where the change is being implemented.

Key Takeaways

- Change management and individual industries (such as Education or Technology) have a wide range of differing, complex and confusing terms and definitions.

- Therefore, to avoid any confusion and unnecessary problems, then it is important to agree on a consistent set of terms and definitions for all stakeholders (such as internal parties, external suppliers, customers, regulators, etc.) covering both Change Management and the industry where the change is being implemented

5 Has sufficient pre-planning work been performed?

> *"Success depends upon previous preparation, and without such preparation, there is sure to be a failure"*
> *- Confucius*

5.1 Introduction

All changes need some element of pre-planning or preparation before the Change Team can start the change 'properly'. The old saying of "perfect planning prevents poor performance" is excellent advice when implementing change.

Unfortunately, it is not uncommon for organisations to jump into starting a change without performing any pre-work or preparation. This means these organisations do not understand the 'personality' or the 'shape' of the change. For example, what has triggered the change? What is the business reason for the change? What is the scope of the change? Who needs to be involved? Who will benefit when the change is fully implemented? Etc. This lack of thinking and sometimes rash behaviour can result in problems, wasted effort and sometimes a large amount of rework. The result is that the change is unsuccessful.

A lack of proper up-front thought and planning is a key reason for change failure.

It is often better to delay the start of a change to complete further pre-planning than to start the change straight away. This could eat into the available timelines, budget and resources, but if good solid up-front preparation work is completed then it will mean the change will run smoother and it will possible to catch up on any perceived delays from starting later. For example, if a firm was to launch a new product, then it would be much better to complete market analysis regarding the offering, the fees, profit margins and what the competition is offering before starting to launch the product. This will avoid any issues with the launch. Likewise, for a major technological change (such as moving an in-house hosted data centre to the cloud) it will be a good idea to perform some up-front analysis on the feasibility, the cost, advantages, disadvantages and possible before jumping in to start the actual data centre migration straight away.

This area of pre-planning is very wide and, to ensure there is some type of focus, then it has been split into five main groupings.

1. The first area relates to some initial thinking that organisations should perform before they even start thinking about making a change. This covers factors such as understanding what has triggered the change, what the business case for the change is, who will benefit from it, how success will be measured, etc.

    If there is any ambiguity or lack of clarity in this area, then the organisation should stop the change and address these points immediately.

2. The second area relates to planning. While is noted that it is unlikely to be able to create a detailed plan at this area stage, an organisation should be able to understand what 'things' need to be changed to make the change happen, how the change will be transitioned into the live environment and pull together some type of high-level change plan.

    If this is not possible, then then the organisation should stop the change immediately and focus on tackling these points

3. The third area relates to the governance structures and processes that need to be put in place. All changes need some sort of controls and governance in place and therefore this must be thought about as early as possible. For example, is there a suitable sponsor nominated for the change? Are there suitable management oversight forums in place? Is there a good Change Manager in place? Are there good communications processes in place? What control processes are in place? Etc.

   If there are any material gaps in this area then the organisation should pause the change and ensure these are addressed as soon as possible.

4. All Changes need a large number of people, teams, groups, organisations, etc. to be involved to allow them to be implemented successfully. This collection of people, teams, groups, etc. is often called the Change Team. This could cover internal suppliers, external suppliers, team members, regulators and so on. Therefore, it is very important at this early stage to identify who needs to be involved and include them in the change as soon as possible. This will ensure they are briefed on the change, know what is required of them and also it will allow them to raise any issues or problems early in the process.

   If there are any unknowns or any ambiguity in these areas then they should be addressed as quickly as possible.

5. The fifth and final grouping is not a pre-planning activity in the strictest sense. But it is important to remember that implementing change is a challenging piece of work and will involve a lot of people working long and stressful hours. Therefore it is important to always say thank you and appreciate people for their help.

The structure of this section is based on a list of questions split into the five groupings listed directly above. Each question focuses on a particular problem that can hinder successful change and then offers some guidance on how this area can be addressed.

INITIAL THINKING

5.2 Is it clear what has triggered the change?

At the start of the change, an organisation needs to be very clear on what has triggered the change.

Firstly this ensures the change has some sort of strategic focus and when implemented will provide some sort of benefit to the organisation and its stakeholders. It is important to understand how the change positions itself with all the other changes in progress and all the other organisational priorities. Organisations do not have an unlimited supply of resources, time and money which means they must focus on 'what needs to be done' as opposed to making changes for the sake of it. There is a long history of organisations starting changes for no apparent reason which wastes time, money and resource as well as being a distraction.

Secondly, it will also help the structure of the change when is it being executed. For example, if the change is triggered by the need to comply with some new legislation by a date set externally by a local government then this will help with key planning dates, understanding what needs to change, who needs to be involved etc.

Thirdly, it is also interesting to note, that the triggers for a change could be altered once the change is running. For example, if the change was to comply with a new piece of legislation and this legislation changes during the implementation then change triggers could become void and the change may now not be required. Therefore it is important to constantly review change triggers to see if they are valid even when the change is running.

If any of these points are unclear, then there is a strong likelihood that the change will fail. The world is littered with failed changes that started without a clear reason or set of triggers.

Change triggers themselves can fit into two very general classifications.

- The first classification is changes that an organisation is forced to make. For example, regulatory change (such as new laws or regulations), political change (such as complying with BREXIT) or technology changes (such as having to upgrade to the latest version of a system).

- The second classification is where the organisation proactively decides to make a change to meet its strategic objectives. For example, executing a change to attract new clients, increase profits, reduce costs, manage risk, improve operating efficiency, etc.

One interesting point to note is that most changes often are triggered by more than one reason. There is often the main trigger for the change which is complemented by some other reasons. Furthermore, once a change is being suggested, then the organisation could 'throw in' some extra items which are along the lines of if the change is planning on doing 'open heart surgery on one part of the organisation then we should look to 'fix the liver and kidney' at the same time? A good example of this is BREXIT where the main trigger for a change was to ensure that organisations could comply with any EU/UK trade deal post-January 2021. But at the same time, many organisations expanded the scope of their BREXIT changes revamp their EU offering, review their EU sales processes and sometimes even think about opening or closing offices within the EU.

However, the key point to stress is that if it is unclear why this change is being made then an organisation needs to stop the change, stand back and ask the question of whether this change needs to be made or not.

Key Takeaways

- If it is unclear what has triggered a change, then an organisation should immediately stop the change and review the situation immediately with the relevant senior management.

- An organisation should not proceed with a change unless it is crystal clear what has triggered the change and how the change supports the organisation's strategy.

- It is also important to constantly review the change triggers during implementation to ensure they are still valid. If not then the change may become void and may not be required.

- Otherwise, the change will almost definitely fail.

5.3 Is it clear what the business case for the change is?

Once the change triggers are clear and understood then a business case needs to be completed to ensure that (a) the change will provide benefits to the organisation and also (b) the change fits within the organisation's overall strategy

Two main types of business cases can be created:

- The first type relates to changes that an organisation is forced to make. For example, regulatory change (such as new laws or regulations), political change (such as complying with BREXIT) or technology changes (such as upgrading to the latest version of a system).

  The business case for these is effectively a 'no brainer'. It is often a case of if we do not do the change then the business may be able to keep running or, if it can keep running, it will be materially impacted in a bad way.

  However, for these changes, it is still worthwhile to understand the cost of the change and the resource requirements because it could distract the organisation from other activities. A good example of this would be financial services which have been under the pressure to implement a large number of changes to comply with new regulations over the last ten years. This has consumed a large amount of money, time and people which has deflected this industry from improving its products, customer servicing and efficiency.

- The second type of business case is where the organisation proactively decides to make a change to meet its strategic objectives. For example, executing a change to attract new clients, increase profits, reduce costs, manage risk, improve operating efficiency etc.

  In this case, a persuasive business case will need to be created to ensure that the change matches the organization's strategy. It is typically normal for the Change Manager to co-ordinate the production of this but the individual aspects of the business case will need to be supplied by the business teams and owned by the Sponsor and Steering Committee.

A business case will usually contain two overlapping or interacting sets of analysis.

- Firstly, quantitative analysis will be required to assess the monetary costs to (a) implement the change, (b) any cost savings as a result of the change, (c) any revenue increases caused by the change and (d) any (if any appropriate) payback periods that are involved.

- Secondly, this quantitative assessment will need to be supported by some type of quantitative analysis which will assess factors such does the change improve the market perception of the firm, does it make customers happier, does it make the company a better place to work, are there any assumptions, are there any risks etc.

Once the business case has been documented then it needs to be approved by some sort of senior forum such as a Board of Directors or some other senior executive management forum.

Mitigation and action

- If it is unclear what the business case or benefits of a change are to organisations then they should stop the change immediately and review the situation with the relevant senior management.

- An organisation should not proceed with a change unless it is clear what the business benefits are how they match the organisation's strategy.

- Otherwise, the change will fail.

5.4 Is it clear who will benefit from the change?

While this question could be part of sections 5.2 and 5.3, it is worthwhile that the organisation clearly understands and communicates widely who will benefit from the change.

Hopefully, this will avoid confusion, rumours and resentment across the organisation. Also, if people understand who benefits from a change then it is much easier for them to link the change to the Mission Statement (see section 4.5) and be motivated to complete it.

However, if it is not possible to clearly define who benefits then there could be issues with the business case (which is discussed in section 5.3). If so then further investigation will be needed to confirm who will benefit.

No change should proceed unless it is clear who benefits from the change.

Key Takeaways

- It is understood who benefits from a change then it will allow the organisation to link it closer to the Mission Statement and be motivated to complete it.

- If it is not possible to clearly define who benefits then there could be issues with the business case

- If so then further will be needed to confirm who will benefit.

- No change should proceed unless it is clear who benefits from the change.

5.5 Is there a clearly defined and agreed set of success criteria?

A change must have a set of success criteria cleared defined and agreed upon by all stakeholders before it starts. This is a key element of implementing change because if the Change Team cannot define what success is then how do the Change Team measure whether a change is successful or not?

Unfortunately, defining success criteria is much harder than one would think. This is because success is subjective with different people and stakeholders having numerous points of view on what success is.

A common definition of change success is that a pre-agreed set of key success criteria (KSF) have been met when the change is completed. This is a good starting point but this area needs to be expanded to make it more realistic and appropriate to the real world.

There are three types of key success criteria.

- The first is 'positive' success criteria, where something good happens. For example, if an organisation performs a change to reduce costs by 5%, then this would be the 'positive' success criteria.

- The second type is 'damage limitation' success criteria. This is where a change is being made and success can be defined by mitigating any downside. Using the example above, if a firm cuts staffing by 5% then this is defined as the 'positive' success criteria for Finance. However, Human Resources may what to include a 'damage limitation' success criteria which could involve ensuring any staff losing their jobs will be treated fairly and supported through the redundancy process.

- The third type is 'constraining' success criteria, which provides some sort of control or constraint around the change to ensure it does not run wild. For example, using the 5% costs reduction example above, there could be a 'constraining' success criteria that state no more than a certain amount of money could be spent on the change because if a large amount of money is spent then it could outweigh the savings being made.

To add more complexity, different stakeholders will have different views on what success is. These stakeholders can cover many different parties such as internal areas but also suppliers, customers, regulators, the general public and many others.

This means that for one change, there could be more than one success criterion. It is fair to say that some success criteria are more important than others. So the best way to combine them is within an overall weighing of 100%. The most important criteria will have the highest percentage and the least important will have the lowest percentage. For example

Stakeholder	Type	Detail	Weight
Finance	Positive	Reduce operating costs by 5%	50%
Finance	Constraining	Not to cost more than £100K	10%
Finance	Constraining	Completed within 6 months	10%
Operations	Damage limitation	No material impacts	10%
Regulation	Damage limitation	Not material impacts	10%
Client	Damage limitation	No material impacts.	10%

The overall aim of the change is to reduce operating costs by 5% within 6 months, not to spend more than £100k implementing the change and ensure there are no material impacts to daily operations, regulatory obligations and client servicing

Therefore depending on what happens, it is possible to assess how successful the change was or was not:

- If the cost reductions were made (within the constraining criteria of £100k and 6 months) but there were material issues across operations, regulatory obligations and clients then the change can be deemed to have been 70% successful. One could argue this was partially successful.

- However, if the costs were not fully made (say only 2% were possible) but (a) it still spent the full £100k (b) it took the full 6 months to implement but (c) there were no material impacts to the organisation's operations, regulatory obligations and clients then could say the change was 65% successful. Again one could argue that this was also partially successful.

- But if the costs were not fully made (say only 2% again were possible) but (a) it still spent the full £100k (b) it took the full 6 months to implement but (c) there were impacts to the organisation's operations, regulatory obligations and clients then could say the change was 30% successful. In this case, one could argue that the change was unsuccessful and perhaps has even made the situation worse than previously.

There are a few other issues worth mentioning:

- Stakeholders have unrealistic expectations. (An example of this could be stating that there should be no operational impacts if costs are being cut by 15%)

- Stakeholders not being able to (or not wanting to) speak to the Change Team about their criteria

- Not having access to certain stakeholders (such as clients or suppliers) to discuss their criteria

- Stakeholders are non-committal or vague about their criteria

- There are conflicts between the different success criteria

If there are any issues in agreeing on a set of success criteria then it is the job of the Sponsor to arbitrate any issues. If they cannot close these issues then it needs to be escalated to their management. This could be a long process with many meetings, going around in circles and re-opening debates and issues that were closed earlier.

The key point to remember is that each change must have a set of success criteria clearly defined and agreed upon by all stakeholders before it starts. Remember if the Change Team cannot define what success is then how does the Change Team measure whether a change is successful or not

Key Takeaways

- It is essential that each change has a clearly defined and agreed set of success criteria because otherwise how is it possible to determine whether a change is successful or not?

- Therefore if a change is running or about to start and there is no clearly defined and agreed set of success criteria then change needs to stop immediately until this resolved

- No change should progress unless it is possible to measure whether it is successful or not.

5.6 Is there a clear vision of the end-state (or what the world will look like once the change is implemented)?

Visions and end states are very 'management speak' which can be an immediate turnoff. However, it is always a good idea to have some sort of vision on how the change will look once it is fully transitioned into live. For example, high-level operating flows, changes to clients, changed suppliers, new products etc.

This vision does not need to be a long document. It was very much along the lines of 'less is more'. It can be a couple of A4 pages or even a single diagram. Some organisations are now using short videos (of a few minutes) where the Sponsor presents the vision and the end-state.

The end-state or vision has several benefits

- Firstly, it allows the organisation to focus on the big picture. If a change is complex or lengthy then naturally the Change Team will get stuck into the detail and it is very easy to lose the bigger picture. Having this vision document ensures people still understand the bigger picture

- Also having a vision would act as a safety net to ensure that an organisation understands the overall change. If it is not possible to document the change on a single page or explain it on a one minute video then perhaps the organisation does not fully understand why the change is required and what is needed to implement it? If there are issues then the organisations will need to address them.

- Thirdly the vision can be used to help with implementing the change. For example, helping with planning, scoping, and organisational design and motivating the Change Team.

- Furthermore, the vision is very good as a communication tool. Remember a 'picture paints a thousand words'. The vision document can be used to communicate details around the change to internal teams, customers, suppliers, regulators, the general public and anybody else who needs to know.

Key Takeaways

- Completing a documented vision of the end-state is a good idea because it will ensure there is a focus, provides a safety net, helps with implementation and is a good communication aid.

- However, if it is not possible to document this vision then this perhaps the change is not fully understood.

- This means further investigation is required to understand the change, what is triggering it, why it is required, what are the success criteria etc.

5.7 Is there an understanding of what the Business Requirements for the Change are?

Once the Change Teams have a good understanding of what has triggered the change, the business reason, why it is required, etc. then the Change Team needs to drop down a level of detail to document the Business Requirements for the change.

A requirement is a distinct need or want to meet the purpose of the change and can be tested (to prove if it has been met). There are two main types of requirements.

- Functional - This is some type of functionality that needs to be provided. For example, all applications for the new product must be made over on our website or an organisation needs to manufacture a specific type of engineering.

- Non-functional – These document all other needs which are not functionality requirements. They can often cover processing times, volumes and service availability. For example, 'the website needs to be able to process 100,000 applications per day' or manufacturing needs to be able to produce 1,000 units per day.

Therefore the Change Team needs to look at the triggers, business case, benefits and key success criteria and then determine what requirements are needed to ensure that the Change is implemented successfully. For example, using a Product Launch then the following requirements may be listed

- The Product needs to cater for the demands of Retail individuals only.

- The Product must be able to be distributed in UK and EU at launch

- Customers must be able to order the product over the organisation's websites as well as the traditional challenges of 'over the telephone' and 'paper order forms'

- The servicing and manufacturing teams need to be able to cope with 100,000 orders on an annual basis

- Etc.

If any requirements are missed then it could problems further down the change implemented because tasks may be omitted, deliveries not identified, cost missed, etc.

Unfortunately, the generation of requirements can be a challenging process. It involves a large amount of iterative data gathering, documenting, reviewing, etc.

Also, requirement gathering is a specialist task and requires explicit skills. For some organisations (or smaller changes) then the Change Manager or business teams could perform this work but for larger organisations (or larger or more complex changes) then specifically skilled individuals (called Business, Requirements or Functional Analysts) need to be employed.

The following points provide a high overview of the process

- The first step is to determine who needs to be spoken to. It would be a good idea for the Change Manager to speak to the Sponsor and Steering Group to see who needs to be involved. From experience, they tend to suggest themselves as well as various members of their teams. They may also suggest speaking to suppliers, customers and industry bodies.

- The second step is to start gathering the requirements. There are various ways of defining requirements. A few of the techniques have been listed below with their various advantages and disadvantages.

Technique	Advantages	Disadvantages
One to one interview with stakeholders	•Allows detailed questions to be asked and often has a high response rate. • People are also more likely to be open and honest on a 1-2-1 basis.	•Very time-consuming to arrange, hold and document interviews.

Focus Groups / Workshops	• They are quick to run than 1-2-1 interviews. • Allows one to speak to a large number of people at the same time. • The dynamics of the group could allow good discussion and output.	• They can be dominated by one or two people which means the outputs tend to reflect their views as opposed to the wider group. • There could be arguments and conflicts in the meeting.
Questionnaires/Surveys	• Quick to set up. • Can be issued to a wide range of people. • People can answer them at their own speed. • Data is collected in a standardised way.	• People may not respond or not answer the questions properly. • People may misunderstand the questions being asked. • If there are errors in the questions then the data will be poor. • It is not possible to go back and ask further questions.
Analysing documentation	• Very cheap and can be quick to do.	• There may not be sufficient documentation available. • It is not possible to obtain people's opinions first-hand.

The actual technique employed depends on the Change being made, the organisation, and the amount of time there is to gather the requirements as well as any personal preference. (A common approach is a hybrid approach where the Change Team initially analyses existing documents and then hold many 1-2-1 meetings to gather specific details. Once this is done, then the

Change Team will hold some focus groups to holistically review the data).

- Once the Business Requirements are documented then they need to review and signed off by senior stakeholders, the Sponsor and possibly even the Steering Committee.

At this early stage of the change (especially for complex and large changes), there will be several unknowns and gaps in the requirements which will need to be filled with guesses, assumptions and estimations. This will allow the change to start but it is important that if any guesses, assumptions are estimates are used then (a) these are identified in any change documentation so stakeholders do not think they are 'real' (b) later tasks are created to investigate these items so they can be formally completed and (c) all stakeholders, especially the Sponsor and Steering Committee, are made aware of them.

However, if it is still not possible to document even a basic list of requirements of what is needed then it is likely that the change is not fully understood. This needs to be addressed urgently because a change should proceed without an understanding of the requirements.

Key Takeaways

- The requirements for change should be documented as much as possible at the start of the change

- The process of gathering requirements is a specific discipline and therefore should only be performed by suitably skilled individuals.

- However, there will be gaps that will need to be filled by assumptions or estimates with tasks in place to address them as quickly as possible. The relevant change documentation needs to be updated to reflect this.

- Furthermore, all stakeholders, especially the Sponsor and Steering Committee, need to be fully away of any gaps in the requirements.

- However, if it is still not possible to document even a basic list of requirements of what is needed then it is likely that the change is not fully understood.

- This needs to be addressed urgently because a change should proceed without an understanding of the requirements

5.8 Has a suitable amount of money been allocated to the change?

All changes will need an amount of budget or money allocated to them. (Sometimes budget is called capital or revenue expenditure). This is to pay for items such as staff, legal costs, materials, office space, etc.

If an insufficient budget is allocated then the change will not be able to purchase or procure everything required. This means corners could be cut, things will be missed or items will need to be removed to 'balance the budget'. The result is that the likelihood of change failure would increase.

However, it is also understood that it is hard to accurately estimate the amount of money required at the start of a change (especially for a complex change). This is because there were many unknowns. For example, issues outstanding, questions around scope that need to be answered, challenges on timelines and also certain parts of the change may be subject to further analysis or feasibility. But some sort of budgetary amount needs to be confirmed for the following reasons:

- The first reason is to set some sort of expectation. This is because senior management will want some sort of estimate of the costs even if it is subject to change.

- Secondly, it will also feed into the business case. All business cases will have some sort of monetary element within them. For example, a comparison of monetary benefits versus the costs to implement with some sort of payback period.

- Finally, from an organisational-wide financial point of view, firms will want to know how much money they are likely to spend in the current and future financial years

However, there are some ideas and suggestions to help Change Teams estimate the monetary amount required in place of all this uncertainty.

- The first thing to note is that any estimate made at the start of the change will be high level and subject to change.

- The estimate could be subject to several caveats such as further analysis or pending decisions.

- The estimated amount could have a level of probability within it to reflect the uncertainty. For example, plus/minus 20%.

- Also, another good idea is that some organisations create separate budgets depending on different scenarios (albeit each with its own set of caveats and probabilities). For example, if option A is selected, then £ABC will be required but if option B is selected then £DEF is required.

- A further suggestion is to look at previous and similar changes made by the organisation to see what was spent because it may give some sort of indication of what was spent previously as opposed to trying to estimate (or even guess) with limited information.

It is also worthwhile mentioning that organisations do not have limitless cash pot for funding change or anything else for that matter. Therefore it may be necessary for the organisation to limit the amount of available money for fiscal reasons. This will put pressure on the change but it is a fact of life. If this happens and it does look like it will cause material issues then it is important the Steering Committee (and other senior management forums) and the Sponsor are fully aware of possible impacts.

As the change progresses, the budget will 'firm up' as the required further analysis is completed, issues are addressed, decisions are made, etc. This 'firming up' could either increase or decrease the monetary amount

Also, the budget could change (both up and down) for other reasons. These could be internal reasons such as mistakes being made, issues being bigger than originally thought etc. These reasons could also be external such as a regulatory date changing, legal requirements being updated, supplier changing their fees etc.

Managing budget changes is not a nice situation to be in but it is a fact of life. These need to be carefully managed with the Sponsor and Steering Committee because it could cause a wide number of problems. For example, voiding parts of the business case or even causing a cash drag on the organisation.

Key Takeaways

- At the start of the change, it should be possible to create an initial budgetary amount, albeit with some known gaps, caveats and a level of probability

- If it is not possible to do this then it could be a symptom of wider issues. For example, the scope, plan, etc. are not fully understood. If so then is recommended that the Change Team investigates the scope, list of changes, timeline, etc. to ensure they understand it in more depth.

- No changes should proceed without at least having an indicative budget

5.9 Does the organisation understand the complexity of the change being implemented?

Not fully understanding the complexity of the change at the start can result in problems, issues and eventual change failure.

Even the simplest change is complex. They have a long list of tasks that need to be done. They will have complex interdependencies. There will be different start dates for different tasks. They will require different skill levels. Furthermore, this complexity will be exaggerated at the start because issues are outstanding and there will be a large number of unknowns. But, as these issues are addressed, then it is hoped that the complexity will decrease. Although it is not that uncommon for the complexity to increase as issues are addressed.

Unfortunately, the world is littered with changes where organisations have dramatically underestimated the complexity of change at the beginning. This has resulted in either the change not being delivered, the scope being reduced or even the change being delivered but with limited benefits. One of the prime examples of this was the various business-wide reengineering changes that were fashionable many years ago. These changes often started well with the ambitious vision that they are going to change the entire organisation within a short period but when the change started to run, the Change Teams discovered issues with the enormity of the change. This resulted in several problems. For example, either the change grounding to a halt or, even worse, it was even a complete failure with the side effects of wasted effort and money

This means organisations need to look themselves in the mirror, at the start of the change, and ask themselves *"Now we have an initial understanding of the scope, timelines, plans, etc., do we understand the complexity of change?"* (This is especially true if the organisation has not done a similar change before).

It is better to challenge oneself now before the change starts, and make adjustments, as opposed to starting the change and encountering major issues when the change is running. If there are concerns then there are several recommendations that can be followed:

- The first one is to ask industry colleagues, who have implemented similar changes to question them about what problems they had and how they managed them.

- The second option is to ask consultants with experience of the change for an impartial and third-party sanity check.

- The third option is to look at case studies on similar changes. These are published in industry and professional journals. They will often provide valuable insights into any challenges and how they were (or were not) resolved.

- The final option is to look at reports on similar changes that have been published.

    However (as noted earlier) most organisations do not complete thorough and honest 'lesson learnt' reviews so either this data will not be available or 'watered down' so much that it is not that useful or even misleading.

    Although having said that, it is not uncommon for large organisations or governments that have encountered massive change failures to complete some sort of post-implementation audit review. These audits are often published which means it should be possible to obtain copies of them and then study them for insights and ideas.

Even if the Change Team do feel they fully understand the complexity of the change then it is still advisable to proceed with caution and constantly review the situation.

Key Takeaways

- Reviewing the complexity of a change before it started a massive safety check.

- If an organisation underestimates the complexity of a change then it could fail.

- Organisations need to look themselves in the mirror and ask themselves *"Now we have understood the scope, timelines, plans, etc., do we understand the complexity of change?"*

- This is especially true if the organisation has not done a similar change before

- It is better to challenge oneself now before the change starts, and make adjustments, as opposed to starting the change and encountering major issues when the change is running.

- Even if the Change Team do feel they fully understand the complexity of the change then it is still advisable to proceed with caution and constantly review the situation.

5.10 All changes will have a large number of problems and the stakeholders must be aware of this?

Regardless of the amount of preparation completed and or the skill of the Change Team, things will go wrong. This is because change is such a complex phenomenon. Therefore, stakeholders need to understand this and be taken along the journey.

The following diagram provides a humorous overview of the human reaction to change.

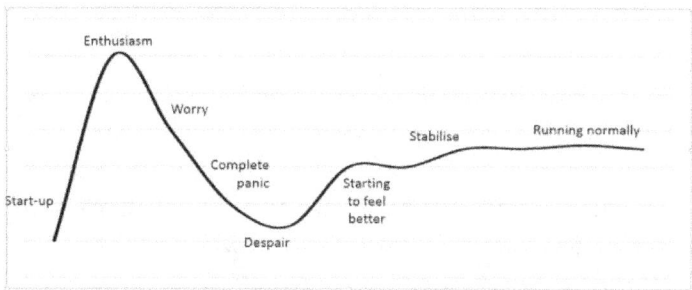

After the change started, there was a large amount of enthusiasm. Several problems were encountered which caused worry, panic and then despair. Once these issues were resolved, things got better, stabilised and the implementation started to run normally.

Therefore, all stakeholders need to be aware of this and understand problems do happen.

If some stakeholders are not aware of this then the Change Manager and Sponsor need to work with them to ensure they understand this.

This awareness can be socialised by (a) ensuring all stakeholders understand the issues around budgets, scope, timelines, etc. and (b) they are constantly updated on progress via either the normal reporting or via one-off reports such as a special meeting, an email or ad-hoc update.

Key Takeaways

- Change is a complex subject and despite having the best plans in place there will be problems.

- Therefore, to manage expectations, all senior management must be aware of this.

PLANNING

5.11 Is there an understanding of what 'things' need to be changed to implement the change?

Once the Change Teams have a good understanding of requirements (see Section 5.7 above) then the Change Team needs to drop down another further level of detail to try and understand what needs to be done to implement change.

In other words what 'things' (such as organisation processes, arrangements, constructs, etc.) need to be altered to allow the change to be implemented. This means that some type of impact assessment will be required and it is important, this is done pretty early in the process because it will help drive planning, cost management and change structure.

This list of items that need to be changed is often called the scope

This scope of work could cover many areas. Using the first requirement in the example listed in section 5.7 above namely "The Product needs to cater for demands of Retail individuals only". To allow this requirement to be implemented then it may need 'things' changed to product specifications, the technologies that support the products, marketing materials, client servicing arrangements, distribution channels, etc.

At this early stage of the change, it will be hard to provide a detailed or specific scope, especially if there are issues or gaps in the business requirements. For this reason, most changes initially look at what needs to be changed and 'plug' any gaps with guesses, assumptions and estimations. This will allow the change to start but it is imperative that if any guesses, assumptions are estimates are used then (a) these are identified in any change documentation so stakeholders do not think they are 'real' (b) tasks are created to investigate these items so they can be formally completed and (c) all stakeholders, especially the Sponsor and Steering Committee, are made aware of them.

However, if it is still not possible to document even a basic scope of what needs to be changed then it is likely that the change is not fully understood. This needs to be addressed urgently because a change should proceed without an understanding of the scope and issues

Key Takeaways

- The scope of a change should be documented at the start of the change as much as possible

- However, there will be gaps that will need to be filled by assumptions or estimates with change tasks in place to address them as quickly as possible. The relevant change documentation needs to be updated to reflect this.

- Furthermore, all stakeholders, especially the Sponsor and Steering Committee, need to be fully away of any gaps in scope.

- However, if it is still not possible to document even a basic scope of what needs to be changed then it is likely that the change is not fully understood.

- This needs to be addressed urgently because a change should proceed without an understanding of the scope and issues.

5.12 Is there an understanding of how the change will be transitioned into the live environment?

Even at this early stage of the change, it is worthwhile having some sort of idea of how the change will transition into the live environment. This will help with the vision, communication, planning and implementation. This transition can cover many areas such as moving offices, changing business processes, launching products, implementing technology, changing staff contracts etc.

There are several different types of transitions.

- One is the traditional big bang approach where the entire change transitions in the live environment at once. For example, upgrading a new piece of software or technology. The transition period is often very short (say an evening or a weekend) but there is a large amount of risk trying to perform all the transition activities at once. The advantage of this option is that the change is implemented at a single but big bang approaches can be risky to implement.

- However, it is becoming increasingly common to use phased transitions. This reduces the risk of a "big bang" but does increase the length of the transition. For example, using a new product launch. An initial test launch could be initially performed with a target customer base with the focus on testing that the product and the support processes work. If there are issues then they can be addressed before any later phases.

- Also, phased approaches are often necessary due to a lack of time to complete the full transition. For example, the author once worked on a large outsourcing change. There were a large number of business activities that had to be transitioned from the in-house team to the outsourcing supplier, and there was not enough time to perform them over a weekend (including even a bank holiday weekend). This meant the transition was split over several weekends spread over several months. This increased the length and complexity of the migration but avoided a risky "big bang" approach.

As noted earlier, having an idea of the transition approach as early as possible will help with planning the change, especially regarding who needs to be involved, the governance structure, workstream structure, costs etc. It will also set expectations with stakeholders (such as the Sponsor, Steering Committee, suppliers, customers and even regulators). It will allow them to raise issues at the start of the change when everything is still very much in the planning stage, then to raise problems when the go-live transition is much nearer.

However, if an organisation or a change, is struggling even to think about how the change could be transitioned into lie at even a high level then it could be a sign that they do not understand the change in sufficient detail and this could be a sign of trouble. If so then it is recommended that the change stops and investigates the change in more detail before proceeding.

Key Takeaways

- Having an idea of the transition approach as early as possible will help with planning the change and it will set expectations with stakeholders (such as the Sponsor, Steering Committee, suppliers, customers and even regulators). They should object at the start of the change when everything is still very much in the planning stage, then when work on the transitions is actually in progress.

- If an organisation or a change, is struggling even to think about how the change could be transitioned at even a high level then it could be a sign that they do not understand the change in sufficient detail.

- This is a sign of trouble and the change should investigate the change in more detail before proceeding.

5.13 Has an initial change plan (even if draft) been completed?

Once the scope (albeit with some gaps and unknowns) is understood by the Change Team then it should be possible to draft at least an initial high-level change plan.

There are many different ways that a plan can be developed. Some of these approaches are complex and others are much simpler. However, the following should be able to allow a Change Team to develop a change plan reasonably quickly.

- Firstly, it is important to identify the task or chunks of work required at a high level. This can be done by reviewing the list of scope items (see section 5.11) and then working out what needs to be done to implement them. For example, if the Change Team is doing a product launch, then the tasks could be market research, design, testing, and then launch.

- Once this list of tasks is completed then it is a case of working out the dependencies between them. In other words what tasks cannot start until another task or tasks are finished. Using the product launch example from above, it will not be possible to start designing the product until the market research is complete or it will not be possible to test the product until it is designed and built.

- Once the dependencies are understood, then it is possible to understand what resources are required. This can cover anything from people, skills sets, technology, suppliers, customers etc. Again using the product design example and in particular the market research task. The change may data on their target audience and competitors which can be 'crunched' to produce the required market research.

- Next, once the resource requirements are included then it will be a case of inserting any critical dates into the plan. For example, for a product launch, one may want to launch the product by Christmas or during the summer holidays. This may result in changing the required tasks as well as their order and dependencies.

- Finally, once all the above actions are completed, then it is possible to understand the critical path. A critical path is the sequence of linked tasks that if any of them are delayed then it will impact the end-date. In effect, this acts as a 'back-bone' through the change which will (a) determine how quickly the change can be made and (b) which tasks must be completed on time to minimise the chance of delays.

Even if a large amount of work is performed, it is unlikely that the first round of planning will create an acceptable first draft of the plan. It is important to note that planning is an iterative process which means it could take time to create an acceptable first draft of the plan. There will be a host of problems and issues that will need investigating and fixing. For example:

- Will it be necessary to delay the delivery of key requirements? For example, launch the product next Christmas as opposed to this Christmas.

- Alternative the change may want to phase the implementation of key deliveries. For example, the Change Team might want to do an initial launch to meet the Christmas or summer dates with a follow-up launch later on.

- The change may want to bring in more resources to ensure deadlines are met such as people with specialist skills. This may incur an extra cost for the organisation or it may be possible to 'steal' resources from another change which could, in turn, impact their deadlines.

- Change Team may need to reduce the scope to ensure deadlines are met. The omitted scope could either be dropped from the change or included in either future phases or moved to another change.

- Plus many others

Also, it is important to note, that even if all the information is available, (which is extremely unlikely) any plan will always include estimates and sometimes even just guesses. For large and/or complex changes it is impossible to fully plan everything at the start of the change. This means there will always be some sort of ambiguity and updating the plan as the change runs. Dealing with and managing ambiguity is a key skill when delivering change.

However, regardless, it should be possible to create some sort of plan that will (a) allow the Change Manager to drive the change forward and (b) provide a steer to the Sponsor, Steering group and other senior management regarding the key issues around the plan and its deadlines.

A final point to mention is that a well-structured plan that is easy follow is a very good communication tool. At its basic level, a plan is just a list of tasks and dependencies which can be quite hard to follow. But, if the plan is structured carefully with some sort of logical flow then it 'can tell a story and this can be used when communicating with all stakeholders. For example, (using the product launch example again) it tells the story as "once the market research is done then the product design to proceed; once the product is designed then it will be tested before the full market launch".

However, if it is not possible to create even a simple then this could be the symptom of something more significant. The lack of planning is a key reason for change failure. If so then further work should be completed to understand the triggers of the change, the reason for the change, the business justification, etc. A change should not proceed without some sort of plan (even if it is a draft with some issues outstanding)

Key Takeaways

- Creating a plan at the start of a change should always be attempted but there will always be issues (especially for the larger and more complex changes).

- It should be possible to define the main tasks or chunks of work, their dependencies, the resources required to implement them, any key dates and the critical path.

- It should also be possible to highlight any gaps, issues or unknowns as part of this change.

- However, if it is not possible to create even a simple then this could be the symptom of something more significant.

- If so then further work should be completed to understand the triggers of the change, the reason for the change, the business justification, etc.

- A change should not proceed without some sort of plan (even if it is a draft with some issues outstanding)

GOVERNANCE

5.14 Does the change have an appropriate Sponsor?

Once the business case has been approved then the organisation needs to nominate a senior member of management to act as the Sponsor (although this role is sometimes referred to as a Change Champion).

The Sponsor's responsibility is to be accountable to ensure the change is implemented successfully. If the change is successful then the Sponsor can take the plaudits but if the change is unsuccessful then the Sponsor will need to take full responsibility. This failure could result in disciplinary action or even sometimes dismissal from the organisation. There are some high profile public sector change failures where there is demand for the sponsor to be prosecuted.

This means the selection of a Sponsor is not an easy process but the items below should be able to provide some help:

- The Sponsor should be somebody who will benefit from the change as part of their normal job. For example, if the change is to improve customer services, then the Sponsor could be Head of Client Services. Likewise, if the change is to improve operating efficiency, then it could be this Chief Operating Officer.

- The Sponsor should also take an active interest in the change. It is not just a case of leaving the change to the Change Manager and team to complete. The Sponsor should be involved actively in the change at all times. This will involve providing support, giving advice when required and challenging the Change Manager and team to ensure they perform the best job possible.

- The Sponsor will need a large amount of personal, professional and positional gravitas within the organisation. This is because they will need to drive the change from the top level. This will cover ensuring there are sufficient resources and support available to the Change Team, providing sufficient challenge to ensure the change is being implemented as effectively as possible, as well as, providing and steer and support to the Change Team plus many other areas.

- The Sponsor would also need to chair any senior meetings concerning the change such as Steering Committee and/or other senior forums.

- The Sponsor will also need to represent the change at other forums such as Board Meetings, Executive Management boards and possibly others.

Therefore, this means a good Sponsor needs to be skilled in several areas; namely:

- They need to have a good understanding of change management as a discipline (such as planning, dependencies management, risk management etc.) This will allow them to provide support to and/or challenge the Change Team.

- They need to be a subject matter expert in the area that's been changed. For example, technology, sales, manufacturing, etc.

- They need to be a good communicator because they will need to sell the change to the wider organisation and motivate the Change Team.

- Lastly, they need to have good interpersonal skills because they will need to address any conflict between staff, any personal issues, motivating staff and dealing with other personal issues.

Key Takeaways

- It cannot be stressed enough that the selection of a suitable Sponsor is essential.

- If the change is successful then the Sponsor can take the plaudits but if the change is unsuccessful then the Sponsor will need to take full responsibility. This failure could result in disciplinary action or even sometimes dismissal from the organisation.

- The world is scattered with failed changes that did not have the correct Sponsor.

- If there is any concern about the selection of the Sponsor then this needs to be addressed with senior management immediately before the change progresses too far.

5.15 Is there suitable senior management oversight and forums in place?

As mentioned earlier, the Sponsor has already been nominated, but there needs to be some sort of wider forum to oversee, steer and challenge for the specific Change being implemented. This is sometimes called a Steering Committee, Project Board or a Change Board (although to try and avoid confusion, this book will use the phrase Steering Committee)

If this senior oversight is not in place then there is a real chance that the change will miss issues and/or not receive the support required which will result in a change failure.

This Steering Committee needs to have a good selection of appropriate members to match the change in progress.

The first two members are the Sponsor and the Change Manager.

But there need to be several other key members to ensure the required oversight, steer and challenge can take place. Therefore it would be advantageous to include representatives of key suppliers (both external and internal) so they can report and be accountable for their deliverables. Likewise, it would also be valuable to include people from the areas that will be benefiting from the change so they are aware of the progress being made as well as any problems. Furthermore, it is always good to include some control functions such as Finance (to confirm monetary spend), risk management and legal. Finally, it may be worthwhile bringing guests into meetings as circumstances dictate such as specialist updates or discussions.

The frequency of these meetings need to be agreed but it is dependent on the specific change. Typically these Steering Committee meetings are only held as and when they are required. For example, when key decisions are needed or there are major issues that need to be discussed. This means it is not uncommon for meetings not to take place for several months. But having said that, it is sometimes worthwhile just booking them every month or so to ensure they are in the diary in case they are needed. If they are not needed then they can be cancelled.

The change also needs to understand what reporting and updates the Steering Committee needs. Typically there will be some sort of 'pack' which is issued several days before the meeting. While there again are no hard and fast rules and what needs to be included, it could include it for issues for escalation, decisions required and a general progress update.

If it is not possible to determine who needs to sit on a Steering Committee then it is a clear symptom that there is a problem with the change. For example, the scope is not fully understood, it is unclear which teams need to be involved, etc. If so then further work is required to address these items so a Steering Committee can be formed. No change should proceed without a Steering Committee (or similar forum) in place.

Key Takeaways

- There must be some type of senior forum to oversee, challenge and steer the change. Otherwise, there is a real chance that the change will miss issues and/or not receive the support required which will result in a change failure.

- The forum (a) must contain the required members (b) meets as frequently as required and (c) receive the correct inputs.

- If an organisation is struggling to determine who needs to sit on this forum then it is probably a sign that the change is not fully understood. Therefore further work is required with the Sponsor on understanding impacts, what needs to change, timelines and who needs to be involved

- No change should proceed without a senior oversight forum.

5.16 Is there a suitable Change Manager in place?

Once the scope, plan and list of people/teams to be involved have been drafted then a suitable Change Manager must be selected. This person is responsible for driving forward the change on a day-to-day basis. (This person can also be called a Project Manager, Programme Manager or Portfolio Manager. Although for clarity and ease of reading, this book will use the phrase "Change Manager").

The Change Manager is an essential role. If an unsuitable Change Manager is selected then the change will fail. Along with the Sponsor, the selection of the Change Manager is one of the two most key important roles.

Therefore, it is important to spend as much time as possible selecting the right person. Similarly, if a change is in progress and the Change Manager is not correct then they should be either replaced or provided further support as soon as possible.

There are several capabilities and skills that Change Manager needs.

- They need a good understanding of managing changes as a discipline. For example, good organisational skills, good planning skills, the ability to manage scope, risk management skills, tracking skills plus many others.

- They should have an understanding of the technical area where the change is being made. For example, if the change is to upgrade a cloud computing environment then they should have a good understanding of technology and cloud computing. Likewise, if they are working in aerospace then they should have a good understanding of this industry.

- Thirdly, the Change Manager has should have a good cultural fit with the organisation that is making the change. Culture is often an overused word and it is hard to define. But the bottom line is, will the Change Manager be able to work with the organisation to make the change happen or will their actions and behaviours be alienate them? If so then the change will fail.

- The Change Manager should be focused on results. Despite all the other points noted, ultimately they are there to deliver a change and ensure it meets the benefits planned.

- The Change Manager should have good communication skills. At a senior level, they should be able to communicate complex issues and updates to senior individuals (such as Boards of Directors, Sponsors and other senior stakeholders). At more junior levels, they should be able to discuss complex change details with technical experts such as accountants, lawyers, and operational staff.

- The Change Manager should also have verbal and written skills.

- The Change Manager should also have good interpersonal skills because they will often need to deal with conflict, negotiation and personal problems.

- The Change Manager should also have good supplier skills because no doubt they will be impacted in some way during the change.

- Finally, the Change Manager should have good customer management skills because most changes could impact clients in one way or another.

Key Takeaways

- The selection of a suitable Change Manager is essential (although this role can sometimes call Project Manager, Programme Management or Portfolio Manager).

- If the wrong person is selected then the change will fail.

- Therefore it is best to spend as much time on the selection as possible.

- However, if there is a change up and running at the moment in the Change Manager is a bad fit then there are two options for the Sponsor or other senior manager. Either (a) the Change Manager is removed and replaced or (b) they should be given more support from either other change and/or the Sponsor.

5.17 Is there an appropriate communication strategy in place?

Some sort of regular communication needs to be produced and issued as and when required. The purpose of this is to ensure that all stakeholders are kept up-to-date regarding progress, issues in progress, decisions being made and also to ensure that stakeholders know what they need to do.

If communication is poor then this could cause problems, result in damaging rumours being formed, create an amount of scepticism and reduce the likelihood that the change will succeed. This means it is important there is effective communication during the implementation.

Communication can be viewed as a two-way process.

- The first process is outbound communication which means there needs to be regular and focused communication regularly to all groups are both up-to-date with the change and also know how it impacts them. Ideally, there should be a single communication that is sent out regularly such as email or updates on a website. Although some organisations are looking at video messages.

However for specific audiences (such as regulators, clients or specific business teams) then bespoke communications may be required to ensure they hear their specific message. This is more work but is important to ensure the 'message' is heard.

- The second part of communication is that stakeholders generally should be encouraged to ask questions about the change. This will ensure they understand it, make them feel involved and provide the opportunity to raise points that may not have been spotted by the Change Team.

    Again, various things can be done that the most common is to have some sort of central mailbox where questions can be raised, tracked and responded to.

    Alternatively (or in addition) the Change Team may want to have briefing sessions where stakeholders are invited to and can ask questions. If this does happen, it is always quite good to get the Sponsor and other senior managers invited because (a) shows support from senior management and (b) they can answer any challenging questions.

    Finally, some organisations will issue regularly updated frequently asked questions that cover any standard queries.

Key Takeaways

- Good, frequent, accurate and open communication is essential because all stakeholders are aware of what is happening.

- If communication is poor or stakeholders are not aware of what is happening, then this could cause problems, result in damaging rumours being formed, create an amount of scepticism and reduce the likelihood that the change will succeed

5.18 Have suitable processes and controls been implemented?

There needs to be processes and controls in place to manage the change on the day to day basis. This will cover many areas such as tracking progress, tracking spending, what documents need to be completed, how to manage risks, location of document repositories, best practices to follow, etc.

Without these processes and controls in place then the change will struggle to track progress and any problems that arise. Good controls also act as a safety net to trap any problems that the Change Team has missed. Therefore the likelihood of change failure will increase.

Most organisations should already have a standard change management set of processes and controls in place. (See sections 4.12 to 4.14 for more details). Therefore it should possible to use this for the change in question. Also, as mentioned in sections 4.12 to 4.14 earlier, it is not uncommon for a change to take the standard processes and controls and then tailor them specifically for the change in progress.

Key Takeaways

- To maximise the chance of a change being successful then there needs to be some type of suitable processes with controls.

- This will ensure that all key tasks are done, progress is tracked, issues are managed etc.

- A good process can be seen as a good safety net to trap issues.

- If there is no process in place then there is a good chance that the change will be chaotic and therefore not succeed fully. In this case, then the Change Manager, Sponsor and Change Team to put one in place.

5.19 Have all issues, ambiguities and gaps have been logged at the start of the change?

Successful change requires the detailed management of a large number of issues. This means it is important to accurately identify these issues and ensure there are logged, communicated and tracked to completion.

The mismanagement of issues is a massive contribution to change failure.

At this early stage of the change, there will be a large number of gaps, problems, questions, unknowns and issues. These could be triggered by items outside the organisation such as waiting for regulatory guidance, or waiting for a political decision to be made. They could also be triggered by internal issues such as waiting to complete the market analysis on a new product or looking to confirm the costs for opening a new office. These issues could impact all parts of the change such as planning, who needs to be involved, timescales, scope plus others. This means they need to be tracked, managed and communicated to all relevant stakeholders.

However, (to be on the safe side) the organisation making the change should ask themselves two questions.

- Firstly *"are we sure that all issues have been logged and that all stakeholders are aware of them and understand their impact?"* If not, then is essential that the Change Manager ensures that all parts of the change team are constantly asking themselves this question to ensure that all issues are tracked and socialised as required. If the Change Manager is nervous that items are not being tracked then they need to challenge the Change Team more assertively and, if necessary, escalate to the Sponsor and/or Steering Committee.

- The second question is to ask itself *"does the list of issues match the complexity of the change?"* For example, if the change is very complex, then the Change Team would expect a large number of issues. If this is not the case then there could be problems. Again the Change Manager must ensure the Change Team review all parts of the change to ensure that all issues are tracked, challenged and escalated as necessary.

Key Takeaways

- This is another safety check before a change starts 'proper'.

- All changes will have a long list of issues, gaps and unknowns at the start.

- Therefore it is good to constantly challenge oneself to ensure all issues, gaps, etc. are noted for future resolution.

- Remember, it is much better to waste a couple of hours of effort at the start of the change to ensure the issue is correct than to proceed and encounter problems that could take a while to address when the change is running.

- As noted above, the mismanagement of issues is a key contributor to failed changes.

WHO NEEDS TO BE INVOLVED AS PART OF THE CHANGE TEAM

5.20 Is it clear what people, teams and organisations need to be involved in implementing the change.

As mentioned before, change is a social activity. It is triggered by people. It is implemented by people. People use it once it goes live.

Therefore, it is important to determine which people need to be involved when implementing the change otherwise it will fail. These people (or stakeholders) can cover a wide range of areas such as parts of the organisation, suppliers, clients and many other parties.

Admittedly, it can be quite challenging to determine who needs to be involved at the start of a change. This is mainly because there is such a wide range of stakeholders that could be involved. It is also hard to understand exactly when they need to be involved. For example, who needs to be involved at the start of the change? When do they need to be involved during the change? Who is responsible for certain activities? Who is accountable for various activities? Who needs to be consulted? Who needs to be informed? Etc.

However, if the Change Manager has a good understanding of the scope and has a good initial draft plan then this should help.

For smaller firms. It may be a case of just listing all staff members, customer types and suppliers, and then assessing whether they could be impacted or not. This will create some sort of list that can be used to contact them to (a) check whether they need to be involved and (b) ask them whether they believe anybody else should be involved. Once this list is finalised, they can be briefed on the change, the impact on them and what they are expected to do.

The larger firms who have many staff members, millions of customers and a long list of suppliers and other external partners to deal, with this approach is impractical. Therefore, some sort of structured approach is required to determine which stakeholders are impacted by a change.

- One option is to work with the Sponsor, impacted teams, other senior management, etc. and establish who would be impacted and needs to be involved. Some people and teams will be obvious whereas others will be less obvious. Also, it is unlikely the Change Team will get an answer straight away but rather be given the list of names to speak to.

- A second option is to look at reviewing similar changes made by the organisation previously to see which teams and people were. They can then be contacted to see if they need to be involved in this change. For example, if the Change Team is performing a change to upgrade a website, and a similar change was completed in the past, then it would be a good idea to try and get copies of the change documentation and review them to see who was involved.

(Many organisations use a tool called a RACI matrix to complete this. RACI stands for responsible, accountable, consulted and informed).

Once the Change Manager and Sponsor has a list of people, they can then contact them and ask the question (a) do they need to be and (b) ask them to think any other people and teams should be involved. This could be quite a circular process but it must be completed properly. Finally, once there is a full (or full-ish) list then it is a case of meeting them, briefing them on the change, making sure they understand the impact to them and ensuring they understand what need they are expected to do.

However, if it is not possible to identify who needs to be involved then the change has a problem and further work is required to understand the change triggers, plan and scope. It would be unwise to proceed very far in the change without knowing who needs to be involved.

Key Takeaways

- Documenting a detailed list of who needs to be involved in the change is essential.

- This list of people could in-house people, suppliers, customers, regulators plus many others.

- Some organisations use a tool called a RACI matrix to record this.

- Changes that do not have this list with almost definitely fail.

- If the Change Manager and Sponsor has a good understanding of the scope, plan and triggers then it should be possible to create a list.

- However, if it is not possible to identify who needs to be involved then the change has a problem and further work is required to understand the change triggers, plan and scope.

- It would be unwise to proceed very far in the change without knowing who needs to be involved.

5.21 Is there a suitable works stream structure in place to ensure the change is delivered?

Once a Change Manager has been recruited then they can start to work with the Sponsor and other key stakeholders to define the change structure. They need to transform the plans, the scope, the people that need to be involved, etc. into a structure that can deliver the actual change.

This is a very important area. Due to the complex nature of change, it needs some sort of structure to control and steer it. If this structure is not in place or the structure is not fit for purpose, then there could be chaos and the change will fail.

For large changes, there will be a large number of tasks and complexities which means a structure of workstreams need to be created to manage and control them. There are no hard and fast rules for defining workstreams, but typically they are defined around chunks of work and/or deliverables required. For example, an operations workstream, a legal workstream or a product development workstream.

Once the workstreams have been defined, then a person needs to be nominated to lead each workstream and ensure it delivers what it needs to. This could be the Change Manager themselves but, depending on the size of the change, then workstream managers may need to be recruited or nominated.

It is also important that these workstreams have controls within them to ensure they deliver what is required. For weekly meetings, regular progress reporting, etc.

Although it is worthwhile noting, that is not that uncommon for the workstream structure to change as the change progresses or moves forward. For example, if a workstream has delivered its requirements then it can be closed down.

Key Takeaways

- At this stage of the change, it should be possible to create a workstream structure covering the 'chunks' of work or tasks required.

- This structure is required to ensure there is some sort of control to manage the complex and chaotic nature of change.

- If this structure is not in place or the structure is not fit for purpose, then the change will fail.

- Therefore, if it is not possible to define the structure in any detail, then the Change Team may have some issues. It would be advisable to perform some further analysis regarding the scope, plan and the people/teams that need to be involved.

5.22 Have the required internal staff been included in the Change Team?

Per the analysis completed earlier, the change should have an idea of what internal people are needed to complete the change. For example, change professionals, technology teams, business teams etc.

However, these people now need to be brought into the change and allocated to individual workstreams with a list of tasks and activities. If these people are not involved (or involved too late) then they cannot do the work required which means the change will fail.

Key Takeaways

- To ensure that any change is implemented correctly then it needs to correct people involved at the right time. If people are not involved or involved too late then the change will fail

- However, if a change is still struggling to understand what people need to be involved then this is a symptom of earlier issues? Therefore further work is required regarding the scope, plan and which people need to be involved.

- It is dangerous to proceed with a clear understanding of who needs to be involved.

5.23 Does the organisation have the required skill sets in place?

Just as a further point to section 5.22 above.

Once it is understood what internal staff need to be involved in the change then it is worthwhile, double-checking that they have the right skill sets. It is much better to find any gaps at the start of the change so that they can be addressed immediately before they cause any issues during the implementation of the change.

Remember, if some person is good at one technology then it does not necessarily mean they will understand a different technology. Likewise, if an individual understands one type of manufacturing approach, it does not mean that they will understand a different type.

If any gaps are noted, then it needs to be addressed as soon as possible. There are several possible options. Extra training could be performed. It may be possible to second in internal subject-matter-experts to support the staff for a short period. Likewise, it may be possible to procure external specialists to provide the missing skills for a short period.

Remember without the right skill sets then the change will fail.

Key Takeaways

- Once it is understood what internal teams are needed, then it is a good idea to do a final 'safety net' check to ensure they have the required skills.

- If they do not then they need to be filled before the implementation of the change starts.

- This can be done in several ways. For example, training, seconding internal experts if available, or bringing in external specialists

5.24 Have all the required external suppliers being engaged in the change.

Per the analysis completed earlier, the change should have a clear idea of what supplier or supplier(s) are needed to complete the change. Therefore they need to be brought into the change so they can deliver what is required. Suppliers must be involved at the relevant times otherwise they may not be able to deliver what is required and the change could fail.

Depending on the change being made then it may require existing suppliers to be involved or even new suppliers to be found. Regardless of this, they will need to be briefed on what they need to do and be formally engaged from a legal and commercial point of view.

For existing suppliers, each one will have a different engagement approach. Typically they might have a statement of work (SOW), contract amendment or change request that needs to be completed, signed and approved. However, for new suppliers, it will be a more complex and lengthy process because it may require a vendor selection process to be completed with new legal documentation and commercial negotiations around cost, liabilities, etc.

This means it is important to have enough time on the plan to complete all this work. But, once this is completed then the suppliers (existing and/or new) need to be included in the Change Team. For example, they need to be included in the structure, their tasks need to be included on the plan, progress needs to be tracked etc.

However, if a change is still struggling to determine what external suppliers need to be involved then this could be a symptom of issues. Therefore further work is required around the scope, plan and which external suppliers need to be involved. It is dangerous to proceed with a clear understanding of what external suppliers need to be involved

Key Takeaways

- To ensure that any change is implemented successfully it needs the relevant external suppliers involved when they are required. If the correct suppliers are not involved or involved too late then the change will fail

- The process of engaging a supplier can take some time to complete a vendor selection process and any legal negotiations. Therefore sufficient time needs to be included in plans.

- However, if a change is still struggling to determine what external suppliers need to be involved then this could be a symptom of issues. Therefore further work is required around the scope, plan and which external suppliers need to be involved.

- It is dangerous to proceed with a clear understanding of what external suppliers need to be involved

5.25 Have the required Internal or intragroup suppliers being engaged in the change.

Per the analysis completed earlier, the change should have an idea of what internal or intragroup suppliers(s) are needed to complete the change. For example, central data centre teams, central marketing teams or central legal teams. These need to be brought into the change so they can deliver what is required.

Intragroup suppliers must be involved at the relevant times otherwise they may not be able to deliver what is required and the change could fail.

Most internal teams will have their standard process for engage-ment. There will be some sort of statement of work or engagement form that will need to be completed. This will then need to be signed approved by the relevant senior management. However, there are several different complexities around working with intragroup suppliers. The request for help may need to be approved as part of a wider prioritisation process because the intragroup team may receive many requests from all parts of the organisation. If the change feels that this is impacting deadlines then the Sponsor will be needed to help push the process forward.

Once this engagement is completed and the work has been prioritised then it should be possible to incorporate the intragroup suppliers into the workstream structure so their activities can be planned and tracked.

However, if a change is struggling to determine what intragroup suppliers need to be involved then this could be a symptom of issues. Therefore further work is required about the scope, plan and which intragroup suppliers need to be involved. It is perilous to proceed with a clear understanding of what intragroup suppliers need to be involved.

Key Takeaways

- To ensure that any change is implemented successfully it needs the relevant intragroup suppliers involved as and when they are required.

- If the correct intragroup suppliers are not involved or involved too late then the change will fail

- Engaging intragroup suppliers can take a while due to internal engagements and prioritisation processes. Therefore the Sponsor may be required to help if this is starting to impact deadlines.

- However, if a change is struggling to determine what intragroup suppliers need to be involved then this could be a symptom of issues. Therefore further work is required about the scope, plan and which intragroup suppliers need to be involved.

- It is dangerous to proceed with a clear understanding of what intragroup suppliers need to be involved.

5.26 Have all required customers been engaged in the change?

Customers may need to be involved in the change and if they are not involved as and when required then it could result in the change failing. It would be very embarrassing if an organisation did not realise that they had to include customers until towards the end of the change and then they had to be quickly involved at the last minute.

However, dealing with customers is much trickier than dealing with suppliers. This is especially true if there is a poor relationship with clients or the organisation is worried about opening up itself in front of its clients.

Therefore, it is important to be very clear upfront about what is needed from the client. For example, is it a process change? Is it a technology change? Do they need to sign new contracts? Etc. Therefore two possible options:

- Initially, it is best to liaise with any internal client-facing teams to understand the best approach. There could be various options. One option is for the client-facing teams to liaise with the clients as an in-between.

- The second is to involve the clients directly in the change themselves (albeit with support from the client-facing teams). However, if they are directly involved in the change, then it will be a good idea to try and isolate them for the rest of the change. This is to ensure they are not aware of any other major issues in a change that can make them uncomfortable and nervous, or cause embarrassment to the organisation.

Also, it is important to have some type of emergency communication plan ready, just in case the customers hear about the change before the organisation has communicated it. For example due to a press leak or something similar. This emergency plan could take emails or press releases that can be issued reasonably quickly or details on whether specific customers need to be contacted on a 1-2-1 basis.

But if a change is struggling to determine what customers need to be involved then this is an indicator of issues. Therefore further work is required concerning the scope, plan and what customers need to be involved in. It is dangerous to proceed with a clear understanding of what customers need to be involved in.

Key Takeaways

- To ensure that any change is implemented successfully then it may need to involve its customers.

- This involvement can either directly include the customers or include them indirect by (say) an internal customer-facing team. It is also a good idea to have an emergency communication plan in place to mitigate the issue if customers hear about the change before they are formally communicated.

- However, if a change is still struggling to determine whether and what customers need to be involved then this is an indicator of issues. Therefore further work is required concerning the scope, plan and what customers need to be involved in.

- It is dangerous to proceed with a clear understanding of what customers need to be involved in. It would be very embarrassing if an organisation did not realise that they had to include customers until towards the end of the change and then they had quickly involved the customers at the last minute.

5.27 Has the required infrastructure for the change been put in place?

All changes will require some sort of physical and virtual infrastructure in place so the change can be delivered. This infrastructure will cost money so it needs to be factored into any costs.

Without this in place then the change will struggle which could result in problems. Therefore if there are any issues with this then it needs to be escalated to the Sponsor and, if necessary, the Steering Committee.

This infrastructure can cover many areas, namely:

- Desks for the team

- Communications methods (such as video conferencing, instant messages, emails and 'phones)

- Meeting rooms, filing cabinets and any other physical premises

- Technological support (such as share areas for documentation storage, laptops, printers, scanners, fax machines, software environments etc.)

- Office supplies (such as pens, paper, highlighters, flip charts, whiteboards etc.)

- Suitable infrastructure to allow staff to work from home (such as a VPN, remote access, etc.). Even in the post-COVID-19 world, there will still be a large number of people who will be working remotely.

- Any tools required including physical tools (such as drills, vehicles, etc.), specialist clothing

Key Takeaways

- All changes need some type of infrastructure to operate. The costs of this will need to be factored into the change costs.

- If there are any material gaps in the required infrastructure then this could cause problems. If so then this needs to be discussed with the Sponsor and possibly the Steering Committee.

- Changes that have large gaps in the required infrastructure will fail.

SAY THANK YOU

5.28 Is the Change Team being appreciated for their work and efforts?

(This question regarding appreciating people for their efforts is a common thread throughout the different stages of implementing change. This means that it appears a few times in this book. This has created some duplication but because this is an important point, then the author believes it is justified).

There is a tendency when planning a change to focus on the problems encountered and not thank people for their efforts and hard work for completing activities.

Changes are stressful, require people to work long hours and can be demotivating if problems are being constantly discovered. Therefore it is important for the Sponsor, Change Manager, Steering Committee members and other senior managers to appreciate the efforts and achievements of the Change Team. For example, completing a phase of the change or agreeing on commercial terms with a new supplier

It makes the team feel appreciated and it also motivates them for the future. It is amazing the positive impact that a simple "thank you" or "well done" will have. This is especially true if it is unexpected and is received from a senior member of management.

Therefore the Sponsor, Change Manager, Steering Committee members and other senior managers should be aware of the efforts of the Change Team and the achievements and send out "thank you" or "well done" messages to the relevant team members. A lack of appreciation can cause tensions and impact future working dynamics.

Finally, another way to provide a reward is to review the positive team member's performance and make this known to their managers. Changes are often not part of the employee's day job and there could be resentment on undertaking additional project tasks which are not going to impact the employees' reviews and appraisals.

Key Takeaways

- Changes can be stressful especially if team members are working long hours and/or there is a constant wave of issues.

- The senior stakeholders need to appreciate the efforts and achievements of the Change Team.

- It makes the team feel appreciated and it also motivates them for the future.

- Therefore senior stakeholders should be aware of the efforts of the Change Team and the achievements and send out "thank you" or "well done" messages to the relevant team members as appropriate.

6 Is the change being implemented in the most appropriate manner?

"It's important to have a sound idea, but the really important thing is the implementation"
- Wilbur Ross

6.1 Introduction

The earlier parts of this book have investigated whether the organisation has the capabilities to implement change generally (such as having the required skills, structures, processes, management, etc.) and also whether sufficient preparation work has been done for the change (remember that "perfect planning prevent poor performance").

Without wanting to state the complete obviously, it is also important that the organisation implements the change most appropriately. For example, ensuring that any new software is developed correctly, any new processes or procedures are robust, etc.

If the change is not implemented in the best method then it will fail. There is a long list of change failures where organisations have had the correct capabilities and have also completed sufficient preparation but have not implemented change correctly. For example, they have cut corners when designing process flows, not fully completed software testing, they have rushed the agreement of critical contracts, etc.

This chapter looks at several problems in this area and suggests possible mitigations and remedial actions.

6.2 How supportive and knowledgeable are senior management?

(This item has been mentioned a few times in this book but the author makes no apologies for stressing it here again because it is such a key element).

It is essential that for a change to be successful, it requires supportive and knowledgeable senior management.

The term "senior management" covers several areas. It covers the Sponsor (which has already been identified as a critical role several times) but also (a) management who could sit on the Steering Committee (b) management who are required to implement the change successfully such as finance and technology and (c) management from suppliers and/or customers who are needed to successfully implement the change.

Firstly is senior management being supportive of the change now it is being implemented? Senior management should provide visible and consistent support for all changes in progress. This covers championing why the change is required, what the change is and who will receive the benefits. Management should also be willing to answer any questions about a change, especially if they are challenging questions that the Change Manager is either uncomfortable with or is unable to answer. This support will provide an environment and culture of focus and urgency to complete the change.

If the Change Manager feels they are not getting sufficient support from the Sponsor, then he should tactfully raise this with the Sponsor and if necessary the Steer Committee and other impacted managers.

Secondly, are senior management knowledgeable about the changes being made? (Remember that knowledgeable management will help steer, guide and challenge the change). It is possible that once a change starts then other technical disciplines may need to be covered and the original management allocated to the change may not have all the knowledge required. For example, if a new office is being opened in a foreign location, then there will no doubt be some complex rules around the legal set-up, financing, staff recruitment, distribution, manufacturing etc. Some of these challenges will not have been known at the start and the senior management allocated may have knowledge gaps.

If the Change Manager is concerned that senior management does not have the suitable skills then this needs to be raised with the Sponsor and Steering Committee as soon as possible. Any knowledge gaps could be 'plugged' by (a) recruiting new staff or bringing in consultants with the required expertise while in parallel (b) training senior management with the required know how. The knowledge must be eventually held within the organisation. Firms cannot continue to rely on (often expensive) consultants to 'plug' any knowledge gaps.

Key Takeaways

- Changes without support from senior management will fail. This is unfortunately a common reason for failure.

- If there are areas of concern in this area, then the Change Manager will need to speak to the Sponsor, Steering Committee as well as their fellow senior managers to try and address this issue. This will not be an easy conversation.

- There are various options to address these problems (such as involving different management or temporarily recruiting experts).

- But if these problems persist then, at best, the change should proceed with caution especially if there are tight deadlines, or, at worse, the change should either pause or slow down until the issue is addressed.

6.3 How well are the Change Manager and the Sponsor working together?

Arguably, the two most important roles when implementing change is the Sponsor (i.e. the executive responsible for the changes being implemented at the senior level) and the Change Manager (who is responsible for delivering the change on the ground).

To increase the probability of change success then there needs to be an excellent working relationship between the two. They should be able to speak freely and confidentially about any issues and problems relating to the change. These problems could relate to internal staff, suppliers customers, etc.

But if there are tensions between the two, then there will be issues. These tensions could be caused by several reasons such as professional issues, personal issues, historic issues that are rearing their head or just a general lack of respect between the two.

If issues are discovered that start to impact the change then they must be fixed immediately otherwise, it will create problems that will contaminate the rest of the change which could be hard to recover from. There are two main options to address these problems

- The first option is that the Sponsor and the Change Manager try and mend any problems so they can work together. It may be necessary to include third-party remediation to try and smooth any issues.

- The second (which is the most common to be fair) is to replace either the Sponsor or the Change Manager. Although, in reality, due to the senior nature of the Sponsor, it is often the Change Manager who is replaced.

The world is littered again with failed changes where the Change Manager and the Sponsor do not work well together.

Key Takeaways

- The Change Manager and a Sponsor is a key working relationship and it must work

- There are many examples of changes failing because of a poor relationship between the two.

- If there are problems then they need to be addressed immediately.

6.4 Are the correct number of issues being raised for the size of the change?

On first reading, this does sound like a strange thing to say or check but there is a hidden logic.

For a complex or large change then it is natural to expect a long list of complex issues to be encountered. This means if the Change Team is working on a large complex change and the Change Team do not appear to have a 'sufficient' list of issues then it may be an indication that the Change Team do not know what is happening, are missing issues, not fully in control or generally underestimating the complexity. If this does happen then it is worthwhile performing a much more in-depth review (or 'deep dive') of the change to understand whether any issues have been missed.

Mitigations and actions

- This is another key safety net check

- If the Change Team is working on a large change then they should have a large number of complex issues.

- If the Change Team does not have this then it could be a sign of problems such as not fully understanding the change or items are being missed.

- Therefore it is recommended that the Change Team perform a deep dive into the changes to confirm all issues have been identified

6.5 Does the change 'feel' like is progressing well?

Most of the processes to manage and track change are very logical and scientific. For example, is the plan on track? Are issues being tracked? Are the budgets being met? Etc.

However, as stressed earlier, change is a social process and is important not to forget this side of the change because it could provide some surprisingly useful insights which will help change to be successful.

Therefore, the Change Manager must take regular 'temperature checks' with all the key stakeholders (such as Steering Committee members, Sponsor, Change Team members, business users, suppliers and customers) to see how they 'feel' the change is progressing. For example, is it going well? Are they happy with the change? Could anything be done better? Is the change progressing too quickly? Is the change progressing too slowly? Etc.

This will provide instant feedback on how the change is going and this 'gut feel' type of feedback can be a good indicator of overlooked problems. It also enhances the relationship between the Change Manager and stakeholders because the stakeholders will feel that they involve in the change and that their views are being taken into account.

There are no hard and fast rules on how regular this feedback should be gathered but typically once a month or even every couple of weeks should suffice. But, it is a good idea to try and obtain his feedback by 1-2-1 meetings because people are always more open and honest on this basis.

Once this 'gut feel' feedback has been received then it needs to be compared against any formal tracking.

- If the 'gut feel' says the change is going poorly or very well and the formal tracking says the same then this is good because everything matches.

- However, if there is a difference between the 'gut feel' and formal tracking then there could be a problem and this needs to be urgently investigated. The difference could be caused by many causes. Either (a) the formal tracking may not be picking up issues or (b) the person who provided the 'gut feel' feedback is maybe overreacting, not aware of all the facts or just being mischievous.

The bottom line is that asking how people 'feel' about a change then it will provide some interesting feedback that could indicate issues and problems that are not obvious. If these are missed then the result is that the change may not be successful.

Key Takeaways

- A good indicator of change problems is to ask all stakeholders how they 'feel' the change is progressing.

- If this 'gut feel' feedback matches the tracking of the change then this is fine but if there is a difference then this needs to be investigated.

- The differences may not be significant but it could be an indicator of problems that, if not addressed, could result in the change failing.

6.6 How well are change issues and problems being managed?

It is always a good idea to review the volume of problems encountered during the change and, in particular, how the Change Team is managing them. Changes will always have a large number of problems and issues, and this list could be longer for larger and/or complex changes.

However, the key point is not so much how many issues there are but how are the Change Team coping and managing the issues? For example, are these issues been identified and assessed quickly? Are they being managed as required (even if it is a case of proactively saying we look at a specific issue at a later date)? Is the ownership of the issues clear? Are these owners proactively managing these issues and ensuring the wider team is kept in the loop? Etc.

If issues are not being managed proactively or issues are being left to drift, then it will cause problems.

These 'unmanaged' issues will often fester into something nasty, which could cause a material impact later in the change. For example, many years ago, the author was working on a change where there was a complex supplier agreement that needed to be agreed and many issues were outstanding. The organisation did not address these issues very quickly and let them drift. By the time they were resolved and the organisation reverted to the supplier, the supplier had decided they did not want to do business with the organisation. This meant the organisation had to quickly find a new supplier very urgently

Mitigations and Actions

- The old saying "a stitch in time saves nine" is so very true here.

- If issues are managed proactively and effectively then it will reduce the likelihood of change failure.

- If issues appear to be left unmanaged or left to drift then the Change Manager will need to take immediate urgent action to address this.

6.7 Are Change Team members working constantly long hours?

Another safety net check is to check whether the Change Teams are constantly working long hours. This will include direct team members, external suppliers, intragroup suppliers and customers.

Change Teams constantly working long hours could be a sign of a problem.

- It could be caused by issues from earlier in the change. For example not fully understanding the scope, misunderstanding the complexity of the change, not having sufficient people on board, problems with planning, poor forecasting, etc.

- Although having said this, there could be no issues and it could be just a reflection of where the change is at. For example, the Change Team could be preparing for a major transition event and a large amount of preparation work is required.

Regardless, working long hours is not sustainable for several reasons.

- At one level, it impacts the work-life balance of staff which will cause domestic, family and personal issues.

- Secondly, it causes tiredness and stress. This can then cause errors, tension between team members, general stress levels increasing, and even potentially people leaving the organisation.

Therefore if Change Team members are constantly working long hours then the Change Manager and Sponsor need to work together with the Change Team (especially those working the long hours) on addressing this. For example, it is possible to re-plan parts of a change to reduce the hours worked? Can tasks be re-allocated across other Change Team members? Can people work shifts (this is becoming more and more common these days? Or can extra people be brought in to support the change? Etc.

Key Takeaways

- While team members constantly working long hours could be due to the stage the change is at, it is worthwhile checking in just in case because it could be a symptom of a problem with a change.

- Also working long hours negatively impact staff work-life balances which in turn will cause personal issues.

- Therefore if there are issues they need to be addressed as soon as possible.

6.8 Is the governance structure in place still fit-for-purpose now the change is up and running?

As mentioned several times, a fit-for-purpose governance structure is required for all changes.

The actual structure implemented is normally designed at the start of the change. It is often based on a pan- organisation process (if one exist) and then tailored to meet the specific needs of the change.

Remember the importance of a good governance structure is that it acts as a control and safety-net to manage issues, problems, delays, tracking, change requests, etc. across the immediate Change Team, internal suppliers, external suppliers and, if appropriate, clients. This means it is important that it is fit- for purpose. Despite the best intentions at the start of change, flaws and errors in the process may be discovered once the governance processes are used in anger.

Therefore, during the implementation of the change, the governance structure needs to be constantly reviewed to ensure that it is for purpose; namely:

- Are issues being missed by the process? And if issues are being missed then it is important to understand why so this can be addressed.

- Is it tracking everything that should be tracked? And if items are not being tracked then the reasons for this need to be understood so they can be addressed.

- Is it providing the reporting required? If there are gaps in the reporting then the Change Manager needs to work with the receivers of the reports to understand what the actual gaps are so they can be 'plugged'.

- Is the change control process working as designed? If there are problems with the change control processes then it can result in many problems (such as scope creep) and therefore these need to be fixed.

- Is the governance process 'too heavy' for the change and organisational culture? If it is then the process could be viewed as cumbersome and a pointless form-filling exercise. This means team members will ignore it and possibly even resent it. The result is that it does not provide the control required and is a recipe for change failure.

- Conversely, is the governance 'too light'? If so then it will not provide the controls required which will mean issues will be missed, problems will not be managed, escalations missed, etc. The result is that it does not provide the control required and is a recipe for change failure.

If any material issues are discovered then these need to be raised immediately. The Change Manager will need to work with the Change Team, Sponsor, Steering Committee and other key stakeholders to address them urgently.

Unfortunately, there is a long list of problems and failed changes that have been caused by poor or inappropriate governance.

Key Takeaways

- If the governance for the change is not fit-for-purpose then it will not control the change as required and it could contribute to change failure.

- If problems are discovered then the Change Manager will need to work with the Change Team, Sponsor, Steering Committee and other key stakeholders to address them urgently.

6.9 Are key decisions being made as and when they are needed?

All changes require a stream of decisions to be made. These decisions can range in size, timing, complexity and criticality:

There will be 'junior' or 'on-the-ground' decisions that the Change Manager and the Change Team will make as part of their day to day running of the change. But there will also be some large key or strategic decisions that will need to be made and it is essential are made as and when they are required. For example, entering/exiting a major supplier agreement, making staff redundant, terminating a major client agreement, etc.

These bigger decisions will need to be made by more senior stakeholders such as the Sponsor, the Steering Committee or even by senior groups, such as the Board of Directors or even shareholders. It is also worthwhile noting that some of these key strategic decisions will need to be approved by more than one set of stakeholders.

Delayed decision making (especially for key decisions at a senior level) is a key reason for changes to fail.

This means that the decision making processes needs careful and proactive planned:

- Initially, the relevant stakeholders must know both (a) that they need to make a decision and (b) by when the decision needs to be made. This means the Change Manager (in conjunction with the Sponsor) will need to ensure the relevant stakeholders are aware and briefed about this. This process is often called 'warming them up'.

- Also, it is worth remembering that more than one senior group of stakeholders may need to make the decision. If so it is important to understand the order of decision making. For example, the Sponsor may need to make a decision first, the Steering Committee will then need to approve it before the Board of Directors makes the final decision.

- All decision-makers will need to be provided with sufficient information to allow them to make the decision. For example, they will need general context about the change (if they are not familiar with it), specific information on why the decision is required, what the actual decision is, and a list of any possible options (including how these options are assessed) and then a final recommendation.

- Senior management will need to be given sufficient time to make the decision. It cannot be a case of presenting the decision to the senior stakeholders on one day and expecting a decision the next day. Depending on the change, decision required and organisation then several weeks may be needed. This will need to be factored into change plans.

- Depending on the feedback from senior management then it may be necessary to revamp and update these options and any recommendations. This time will also need to be factored into change plans.

- Finally, the Sponsor, Change Team, Change Manager and other key stakeholders will need to be available to reply quickly to any questions raised by the senior management.

(Using a simple example to illustrate these points. When a new strategic supplier is selected it is often a key decision that could even require the Board of Directors to approve. If so, they would need sufficient time and information to (a) understand the background to this change (b) why the supplier is needed (c) the list of possible suppliers assessed by functionality, timeline, commercial and cultural fit (d) an outline of how the different suppliers were assessed such as request-for-tender was complete which was marked up an in-house team of subject matter expert and (e) what the final recommended supplier is with supporting reasons).

Mitigation and actions

- Decision making (especially at the strategic or senior level) is key and must be made timely.

- The world is plagued with many failed changes which were caused by delayed or slow decision making.

- Some decisions can be made within the Change Team and should be easier to manage.

- However, more key decisions will need to be made by senior stakeholders. These must be made promptly. This means it is essential that the decision-makers are (a) aware they need to make a decision (b) know by when they need to make and (c) are provided with sufficient data/information to allow them to make the decision.

6.10 How well is resistance being identified and managed during the change?

All changes will have some sort of resistance and pushback. This could come from many different sources. Internal staff such as those directly impacted by the change could resist the change. Even any internal staff indirectly impacted by the change can provide a certain amount of push-back. Finally, resistance may even come from suppliers, customers or the general public.

There is a historic tendency aggressively crush resistance or at least suppress it as much as possible. However, resistance is a good insight into the validity of the change being made. It is often raised by people at the 'coal face' who may see issues with the change that the Change Manager, Change Team and other involved stakeholders are not aware of.

This means that resistance must be identified and managed appropriately for two reasons. Firstly if the reasons for any resistance are understood and addressed then it should improve the likelihood of change successful. Though, secondly, if it is not managed appropriately then it could fester and evolve into a major issue that could threaten the success of then change.

There is a long list of changes that organisations have struggled to implement change successfully because they have not proactively managed resistance effectively.

This means that the Change Team (in particular the Change Manager) should actively look for signs of resistance across the change and then take steps to manage it. Unfortunately, this is a lot easier to say than do but there are some different ways of spotting resistance. For example:

- People's actions and behaviours are a good indicator of resistance. For example, do staff look motivated, are they proactively providing input into the change (as opposed to sitting at the back and saying nothing), do they appear negative, have their behaviours changed recently, etc. If this is true then Change Team members may be harbouring some resistance and it would be a good idea to speak to them about it.

- Secondly, the Change Manager could proactively ask people involved directly and indirectly involved in the change about resistance. These points could be raised either in teams meetings, on a 1-2-1 basis, via email, etc. For example, are they worried about the change? Do the Change Team have any concerns? Do the Change Team think the change could be run better? Do the Change Team think errors are being made? Etc. If anything is raised then the Change Team need to act upon it.

Once resistance has been identified then the Change Team needs to understand the real cause of resistance before it can be managed.

- This is much harder than it sounds because people do not often present the real reason when asked. Therefore deep and very tactful questioning is required to try and dig into the detail.

The author once worked on a change to transfer offshore administration activity to low-cost regions to reduce operating costs. There was a large amount of resistance which had a common theme saying it was a bad idea, it would not work, and it would negatively impact clients and would generally be a disaster. However, after more tactful questioning, it became clear that the real reason was none of these. People were more worried about losing their jobs, their friends losing their jobs and the organisation changing considerably once the offshoring is completed. These were valid points that had to be addressed as part of the change.

- Secondly, people need a safe space to raise and discuss resistance. If they feel threatened, scared or worried about being punished or persecuted then they will not raise any resistance and it will continue to fester. There are different ways that a safe space can be configured.

  Resistance can be raised anonymously via email, instant messaging or another electronic medium. However, some people will be nervous about documenting their points because they could worry that it could be used against them in the future.

  However, it is much better to undertake these types of discussions on a 1-2-1 basis. These can be either face-to-face, over the telephone or via video conference. People tend to be much more open on a 1-2-1- basis. It also allows the Change Team to ask deeper questions tactfully regarding the points raised.

  Regardless of the approach, the Change Manager will need good soft and interpersonal skills so they can ask the correct questions which allow the required information to be obtained without making people feel threatened and/or nervous.

Once the resistance is understood then it is important to assess it so its causes are understood. This will then allow it to be managed most appropriately.

- Remember that most resistance comes from people at the 'coal face' who are doing the work that is been changed. Therefore any resistance will often be valid and could improve the chance of success if addressed.

- One of the main reasons for resistance is poor communication. For example, misunderstandings around what the change is, how it is been implemented, who receives the benefits and how it fits the overall organisation. If this is the case, this could be addressed by better, more relevant and more frequent communication.

- The resistance could also highlight issues with the change itself. For example, tasks are missing, timelines are too ambitious, certain individuals need to be included in the change, certain people are not doing a good job, the scope is wrong, etc. Again once raised these items can be addressed.

- However, there is also the unpleasant case where there are some individuals who are naturally disruptive and like stirring up trouble for the sake of it. This can be human nature to a certain extent.

Once the relevance is understood then it can be managed; namely:

- This could cover altering the change to fix the issues uncovered by the resistance. For example, changing timelines or including different people.

- It may also be a case of continuing as previously but explaining to the people who raised the resistance why no action was taken, that their issues were listened to and encourage them to continue to raise points in the future.

- Finally, it may be necessary (despite how unpleasant it is) for people who are deliberately making trouble to be either (a) told to change their disruptive behaviours or (b) remove them from the change.

Key Takeaways

- All change will have resistance but is important that any resistance is understood and managed.

- If it is ignored then it will fester and then cause further problems which could be disastrous for the change.

- Therefore it is important that Change Teams actively search out resistance, understand its cause, assess its impacts and then manage it accordingly.

6.11 How much re-planning is taking place during implementation?

All changes will require a certain amount of re-planning during their implementation. This can be caused by several reasons. For example, previously known gaps in the scope being resolved, earlier issues being addressed, analysis being completed, etc. They can also be caused by external factors such as suppliers changing dates, regulators changing dates or political dates changing. For example, for those who worked on BREXIT, they would have had done a large amount of re-planning as the UK and EU exit dates constantly changed during 2019 and 2021.

However, if there appears to be a constant re-planning of dates (especially if this covers a large number of tasks) then this could be a symptom of bigger problems. For example, poor original planning, lots of unexpected issues appearing, ongoing issues with suppliers, underestimating the complexity of the change, etc.

If this happens then it may be worthwhile stepping back to review the change, and then possibly re-plan either parts of the change or the entire change itself.

Key Takeaways

- Re-planning is a necessary part of implementing change.

- But if there is a constant flow of plan changes then this could be an indication of something more serious.

- If so then it would be worthwhile for the Change Manager in conjunction with the Sponsor and Change Team to completely review the change it is entirely

6.12 How effective is the stakeholder communication strategy?

For many reasons, all stakeholders must be aware of what's happening in the change. All stakeholders need to understand how the change will impact them. Stakeholders may need to do something as a part of the change. They may also notice issues that need to be addressed. And, finally, they generally may want to know what is happening.

Communication can be viewed as a two-way process.

- The first process is outbound communication which means there needs to be regular and focused communications issues to all groups to ensure they are both (a) up-to-date with the change and also (b) know how it impacts them.

  Ideally, there should be a single communication that is distributed. Though for specific audiences (such as regulators, clients or specific business teams) then bespoke communications may be required to ensure they hear their specific message. This is more work for the Change Team but is important that each stakeholder hears the message that is relevant to them.

  The actual communications can be issued using a variety of sources such as face-to-face meetings, presentations, emails, pre-recorded videos, etc. But it is important to choose the correct medium for each stakeholder group. For example, an organisation's largest institutional client would rather have a written or verbal update as opposed to receiving a pre-recorded video message.

- The second part of communication is that stakeholders should be encouraged to ask questions, raise issues, etc. about the change. This will ensure they understand it, make them feel involved and provide the opportunity to raise points that may not have been noted by the Change Team.

   Again, various things can be done that the most common is to have some sort of central mailbox where questions can be raised, tracked and responded to. Alternatively (or in addition) the Change Team may want to have briefing sessions where stakeholders are invited to and can ask questions. If this does happen, it is always quite good to get the Sponsor and other senior managers invited because (a) shows support from senior management and (b) they can answer any challenging questions.

   Finally, some organisations will issue regularly updated frequently asked questions that cover any standard queries.

If communication is poor or stakeholders are not aware of what is happening (or even misunderstand what is taking place) then this could cause problems, result in damaging rumours, create an amount of scepticism and reduce the likelihood that the change will succeed. This means it is important there is effective communication during the implementation.

Key Takeaways

- Good, frequent, accurate and open communication is essential because all stakeholders are aware of what is happening.

- This covers both (a) outbound communication to provide updates etc. plus (b) allow stakeholders to raise inbound communication into the Change Team to allow them to raise issues and questions.

- Remember that it may be necessary to perform different communications approaches for different stakeholder groups.

- If communication is poor or stakeholders are not aware of what is happening, then this could cause problems, result in damaging rumours being formed, create an amount of scepticism and reduce the likelihood that the change will succeed

6.13 Are stakeholders hearing about problems with the Change from people outside the Change Team?

This question is a supplementary question or an extension to the point covered in Section 6.12 earlier. It is also very similar to the question covered below in Section 6.16 (although section 6.16 is very much focused on poor customer communication).

If stakeholders (such as the Sponsor, Steering Committee, Change Team, Business users, suppliers, etc.) are hearing about the updates to the Change from outside the Change Team then this could result in issues when trying to implement the change which will hinder its success. For example:

- The Change Manager and the Change Team will lose credibility with the affected stakeholders. These stakeholders will ask the questions: why did we not hear about this update from the Change Team? Are the Change Team incompetent? Are the Change Team not in control of what is supposed to be going on? Are the Change Team withholding updates or not telling everybody the full picture? Etc.

Once creditability has been lost then it is very hard and often impossible to recover from.

- Secondly, the updates that could be circulating could be wrong. They could relate to problems that do not exist, exaggerate minor problems into something more serious or even understate major issues into something far less serious.

This will create rumours, nervousness, (depending on the seriousness) sometimes panic or give the impression that things are progressing better than they are.

- Thirdly, the updates could be vague and misleading as well as having gaps.

Again, this will create rumours, nervousness, sometimes even panic or even give the impression that things are progressing better than they are.

- Finally, the specific message that is given to each stakeholder could be wrong or inappropriate. Not wanting to sound like a political spin doctor, each stakeholder must hear what is relevant to them. Otherwise, they may misunderstand what is happening which could result in unnecessary panic and tension which will require attention to manage.

For example, if a problem that has been discovered which could be a major potential issue but needs further investigation then the message to senior stakeholders would be along the lines of "major issues been uncovered that could be possibly material – it is under investigation - will report back with impact and options within 1 or 2 days – but let the Change Manager know if you have any questions". However the message to the Change Team members who need to fix the problem could be similar to "a possible major issue has been discovered – will need to report back to senior management within 1 or 2 days – therefore meeting book to discuss impact and options".

Therefore if there is unexpected communication happening then the Change Manager needs to address it immediately. For example:

- The Change Manager needs to send a communication to all stakeholders to acknowledge that there has been some 'misleading' communication that is currently being investigated and further updates will be issued within a short period (say 2 or 3 days maximum). This will demonstrate to the wider stakeholders that the Change Manager has recognised the problem and has taken proactive actions to ensure they are in control of the situation.

- The Change Manager (probably with Sponsor support) will need to find out who (or whom) is issuing these misleading communications. Once the source (or sources) have been found then (a) the Change Manager needs to determine why these updates are being sent because it could be due to a flaw in the Communications Strategy or they are just being mischievous and then (b) tell them to stop sending out the message unless it is co-ordinated with the Change Team.

- Finally, (even if there does not appear to be a flaw in the Communications Strategy suggested in section 6.12), then it may still be advisable to review the strategy to see if there are any problems. For example, are more regular updates required? Are more specific updates required? Are stakeholders receiving all the updates that they required? etc.

All stakeholders must receive updates (regardless of whether they are good, bad or just neutral) from the Change Team. Otherwise, the Change Team could lose control of what is happening which will cause problems with creditability, incorrect information being spread and inappropriate messaging for specific stakeholder groups. This will result in real challenges in implementing any change successfully.

Key Takeaways

- All stakeholders must receive updates (regardless of whether they are good, bad or neutral) from the Change Team. Otherwise, the Change Team could lose control of what is happening which will cause problems with creditability, incorrect information being spread and inappropriate messaging for specific stakeholder groups.

- This will result in real challenges in implementing any change successfully.

- If this is happening the Change Manager (possibly with Sponsor support) will need to determine why this is happening and take immediate actions to stop it from continuing.

6.14 How well are the external suppliers being managed?

All firms rely on suppliers for some part of their operating model. For example, organisations with use suppliers for accounting services, technology hosting, distribution of products, providing staffing plus many others. Therefore, if a change is being made is likely that the supplier needs to change something. For example, adding a new service, changing an existing service, removing a service, etc.

(The scope of external supplier involvement should have been completed in the earlier change preparation work. This should mean the external supplier should be aware of what is required).

This means effective supplier management is an essential part of helping a change be successful. There are a large number of changes that have failed because there have been problems with managing suppliers.

However, some hints and tips can help:

- Firstly, the Change Team need to track what the supplier is doing. For example, are they doing what they are committed to? Are there any problems anticipated? Are they providing value for money? Is the required quality being delivered? Etc.

    If there are problems then this needs to be addressed quickly and escalated both internally and with the supplier.

- Are there any cultural differences between the customer and supplier that is causing problems? For example, a very large supplier dealing may be working with a much smaller customer or vice versa. The smaller firm can be quicker and nimble making decisions but the larger firm will naturally be slower because of its size.

    This needs to be identified and managed because it will cause a conflict between the two organisations. For example, the Change Team need to ensure there is a long time for decision making and provide more support if required.

- Are there issues with time zones? Because if there are then it could cause problems.

    One of the best ways to manage this is to define clear processes for handing work back and forth. It would also be worthwhile to have regular tracking and handover meetings to ensure all parties speak regularly. To create some sort of 'togetherness', these meetings should be scheduled at different times so the same people do not always have the same early mornings or late evenings.

- Another area that has caused problems is how much proactive management of suppliers is required by the Change Team? It often feels like the customer is running the change, not the supplier.

If this is the case, (and it is not possible to get another supplier in the required timescales) then there are some mitigating options. Firstly, regular tracking meetings with tight reporting should be arranged to track the progress of the supplier. Secondly, this issue should be escalated both internally and with the supplier's management. Finally, the supplier could also be asked to provide further staff (at no further cost) to ensure they can proactively manage the changes.

- Another problem is, if there are multiple suppliers on a change, then each of the suppliers could appear to blame each other for any problems or just do not appear to want to work together. This 'blame game' can take place between both external and internal suppliers. It is important to get suppliers working together otherwise it will cause issues with the change.

This mean, the Change Team needs to proactively ensure that each supplier is clear on what they need to deliver and how this links to the rest of the change. In addition, regular and proactive review meetings with all suppliers should be held to track progress together to allow problems to be discussed upfront so they can be immediately addressed which should avoid any 'finger pointing' and blame passing.

Using an example to illustrate this. The author worked on a technology change where one supplier was delivering the front end web screens and another supplier providing the back end application and database. There was a concern that this split of work would cause issues. Therefore clear documentation on, both (a) how the front and back ends would work and (b) how they should integrate was produced. Regular progress meetings between both suppliers were held to ensure progress was tracked, issues were managed and both suppliers worked together.

- One of the other problems with suppliers is them not feeling part of the wider Change Team. They often feel that they are outsiders.

While technically this is true and it is not always possible to involve them fully due to commercial and confidentiality reasons, it is a good idea to involve them as much as possible to make them feel part of the change. For example, include them in team meetings. Invite them on-site as much as possible, discuss problems with them, even invite them to team social events, etc.

There is a long list of change failures caused by poor external supplier management. This means that if any problems are identified then they need to be managed immediately.

Key Takeaways

- All organizations rely on external suppliers to provide a part of their service

- This means if a change needs to be made then these external suppliers will need to be involved and make a change themselves.

- To maximise the likelihood of change success, external suppliers must be managed effectively.

- There is a long list of change failures caused by poor external supplier management.

- This means that if any problems are identified then they need to be managed immediately.

6.15 How well are intragroup or internal suppliers being managed?

Most medium and (especially) large organisations will use a different part of the organisation to supply a part of the operating model. For example, a central technology team, a central legal team, a central human resource team, etc. These arrangements are often called internal or intragroup suppliers.

This means if a change is being made then these intragroup service providers will need to make a change themselves. For example, adding a new service, changing an existing service, terminating service, etc. (The scope of intragroup supplier involvement should have been completed in the earlier change preparation work. This should mean the intragroup supplier should be aware of what is required).

Consequently, the effective management of internal suppliers is an essential part of making a change successful. Again, there are numerous examples of failed changes that did not manage the internal and intergroup suppliers effectively. There are several areas this can be done.

- Firstly, the Change Team need to track their progress. Are they doing what they are committed to? Are there any problems anticipated? How are they coping with issues? Is the quality been delivered as required etc.? Etc.

  If there are any issues are being experienced then they need to be proactively managed immediately. It may also be necessary, to escalate them to the Sponsor, Steering Committee and whoever manages the offending Intragroup team.

- Also while the intragroup team is part of the same organisation, there could be cultural differences that could cause issues. Intragroup suppliers are always perceived to be 'deep inside' the organisation and isolated from the realities of dealing with clients, making money and dealing with the 'real world'. They also have different working processes around requesting work, prioritisation and cross charging. These can often be perceived as slow, job's worth and bureaucratic. They will also have different success factors. For example, the central technology function's main objective is to maintain the data centre (and its software); it is not to deliver the change.

Although this is unfair. It is often a case of having different ways of working and objectives. To operate cohesively the Change Team will need to alter their behaviours to ensure they comply with the intragroup function's processes and ways of working.

- There could be issues with time zones, which need to be managed. One of the best ways to cope is to ensure there are clear processes for handing work back and forth between the teams. It is also a good idea to hold regular tracking and handover meetings for all parties. To keep the relationship fair, the times for these should be rotated to ensure no team is constantly doing early mornings or late evenings.

- Another problem is how much proactive management of the intragroup team is required by the Change Team. Changes that require a lot of proactive management tend to struggle. It often feels like the Change Team is running the intragroup team's work as opposed to them doing themselves.

  If this is the case, then there are some options. Regular tracking meetings with tight reporting should be arranged to track progress and to ensure issues are managed quickly. Any issues should be escalated both (a) to the Sponsor and Steering Committee and (b) to the management of the intragroup service supplier.

- Another problem is that intragroup suppliers often blame each other if there are multiple suppliers involved. (Although, as mentioned above, this 'blame game' can take place between both external and internal suppliers). It is essential to get suppliers working together. Therefore, the Change Team needs to ensure that each intragroup supplier is clear on what they need to deliver and how this links to the rest of the change. Regular review meetings with all impacted suppliers should be held to track progress, ensuring they work together collectively and avoid any 'finger pointing'

- Similarly to external suppliers, intragroup suppliers often do not feel part of the wider Change Team. They often feel that they are outsiders. Technically this is true and it is not always possible to involve them fully due to commercial and confidentiality reasons. However, it is a good idea to involve them as much as possible to make them feel part of the change. For example, include them in team meetings, invite them on-site and maybe even hold social events with them.

There is a long list of change failures caused by poor internal or intragroup supplier management. This means that if any problems are identified then they need to be managed immediately.

Key Takeaways

- All organizations (especially medium and large ones) rely on intragroup suppliers to provide a part of their operating model.

- These intragroup suppliers could be spread across different locations, parts of the organisation, time zones, etc. They could also work in many different methods.

- This means if a change needs to be made then it will need to involve these intragroup suppliers.

- Therefore any involved intragroup suppliers must be managed effectively when a change is being

- There is a long list of change failures caused by poor intragroup supplier management.

- This means that if any problems are identified then they need to be managed immediately.

6.16 How effectively are customers being managed?

All organisations have customers and the range of customers can vary enormously. These can be external customers such as a commercial organisation having paying customers, a charity having its beneficiaries, a government having its voters, etc. They can also be internal customers such as a central technology data centre team having many internal teams using their services.

Depending on the change being made then the customers may need to be involved. This is because the client(s) may have to alter something themselves. For example, change their operating processes, sign new legal documents, be transferred to a new product or service, or even in some cases be offloaded.

Even if customers are not impacted directly then it is often good service to keep them updated regarding the change being made. Customers should hear about changes from the organisation themselves because it gives the impression of being in control, on the front foot and being innovative. It can be awkward and sometimes embarrassing if customers hear about changes either from the competition, via market rumours or through the press. This creates a certain amount of distrust and prompts the client asking "why did you not tell us about this?" (The scope and the impact to customers should have been agreed upon in their earlier preparatory analysis. Also, as part of this, an approach on how to involve clients should have been confirmed. For example, does the Change Team involve customers via the organisation's internal client services team or are the clients involved directly).

The mismanagement of clients is another key reason for change failure. These challenges can be exaggerated if there are other non-change related problems with the client. For example, service problems, legal disputes, the client is just unhappy, the client threatening to leave, etc.

Therefore, clients will need to be managed carefully and there are some ways that this can be done.

- Firstly, it is important to ensure the client understands why the changes are being made. In effect, they need to buy into the change.

    Therefore the Change Team will need to spend some time with them to explain the background to the change, the benefits to the clients, the benefits to the organisation, etc. Otherwise, they will not understand the change, probably complain a large amount and they could even ultimately refuse to make any or delay making the changes required at their end. This could impact the success of the change.

- Secondly, the client needs to clearly understand what they need to change. For example, do processes need to change? Do they need to sign new or updated legal documents? Do they need to make technology changes? Etc.

    This is essential to ensure that they have sufficient notice to make any changes required. If they are told late in the process, then they may not have sufficient time to make the change especially if it requires major rework such as process or technology changes.

- Clients need to be supported by a clear and robust client communication process. This process can be viewed as a two-way process.

Firstly there should be regular outbound and focused client communication to ensure all impacted clients are aware of the state of play of the change. The approach on this often depends on the change and the type of customers.

- For retail clients, it is normally best to have some sort of standard regularly issued communication supported by a set of frequently-asked-questions.

- For larger commercial, institutional or government clients, then it is not uncommon to issue some direct bespoke communication that can be sent as and when required. This communication can be supported by some face-to-face meetings to allow questions to be asked and further clarification to be given.

The second part is that there needs to be some sort of inbound communication process. This will also clients to raise clients and suggest feedback. Again, the structure of this depends on the change and the type of customers.

- For retail customers, most organisations will have some sort of Client Services Call Centre and any questions should be directed towards this. This can be supported by a central email box and social media stream for customers to raise questions.

- For institutional clients, there may be a dedicated client team or a set of account managers, and any questions can be fed through them. Again, it is not uncommon to have a central mailbox or a social media feed as well.

- Finally, if there are any issues or problems with the client(s) then these need to be escalated immediately to the Sponsor, Steering Committee and the senior management who manage the client relationships. They will need to be addressed urgently because the change is impacted or, even worse, the client relationship deteriorates.

Mitigations and actions

- If clients are materially impacted by a change then they need to be involved in the change.

- Customers can be either external or internal.

- The poor management of clients is a key contributor to change failure.

- However, this can be complicated if the client needs to make major changes and/or there is a poor relationship between the organisation and the client(s).

- This means clients need to be involved quickly as possible to ensure they (a) understand the background to the change and (b) know what they need to change.

- This involvement will need to be supported by a robust two-way communication process

- Finally, it is important that any issues encountered are escalated to the Sponsor, Steering Committee and the senior management who manage the client relationship. This should hopefully reduce the change of change failure and negatively impact the client relationship.

6.17 How well are the human aspects of the change being managed?

As noted a few times earlier, change is very much a social process. Remember change is triggered by humans, it is implemented by humans and it is delivered for the benefit of humans.

Therefore, it is important to manage the human aspect of the change. The poor management of this will result in a change failure. There are various examples of change problems and failures that have been caused by teams not working together, team members not working with each other, individuals falling out, etc.

These human aspects cover a range of items like showing sympathy, showing empathy, being patient, being tolerant, having good communication skills (which is discussed in depth in others of this book), employing good listening skills, treating people with respect, etc.

If managed properly then these skills help build trust, create integrity and develop long term working relationships. It will also help build good team solidarity and help with the management of resistance, suspicion and the fear of change. But if they are not managed well then it can cause tension, stress, hostility, etc. which can result in both (a) change implementation issues or even complete failure and (b) an unpleasant, nasty and toxic working environment.

Therefore, like all aspects of change, this area needs proactive management:

- The Change Manager needs to constantly keep looking for possible human aspect issues within the team. These can be observed in several ways. For example, people not contributing, people being isolated from the rest of the team, visible tension between people on the team, open hostility, changing behaviours, staff taking increased sick leave, etc.

- As well as trying to spot problems, it is also worthwhile for the Change Manager to speak to other people to see if they have noticed problems that are not that immediately visible.

  This means it would be a good idea to speak to team members on a 1-2-1 to see if problems are happening. People are always much happier to speak more openly and honestly on a 1-2-1 basis than formally or within a wider group.

  Likewise, it might be worthwhile speaking to people outside the Change Team (such as other colleagues, suppliers not involved in the change etc.). This can be useful because they may have a different perspective and see things that the Change Manager cannot always see. Again it is best to perform this on a 1-2-1 basis because it allows people to be open and honest.

- If issues are identified then they need to be addressed urgently and proactively otherwise they could fester into something nasty which (as mentioned earlier) could both (a) impact the change and (b) also could cause issues to the impact staff such as stress, sickness, de-motivation and resignations.

  There are some different ways that any issues or problems can be tackled. Firstly it is important to understand what the issue is. Is it a simple personality difference? Or are staff being bullied? Or could it be something like people don't like sitting next to certain individuals? Or is it that some people seem to be treated differently from others? Etc.

- Once the reasons causing the problems have been found then they can be addressed. Again there are many options for this.

The first is to speak to individuals who are involved either collectively or on a 1-2-1 basis. All parties need to understand the problems their actions are causing on both the change and other members of staff. The Change Manager may need to act as some sort of arbitrator to help them work through the issues.

Depending on the situation then some more forceful action may be required. If a member of staff's behaviour is caused issues then they may be told that they must change their behaviours because it is adversely impacting other team members and the change holistically.

Another alternative is to change the structure of the problem to reduce the issues. This could involve moving staff onto different tasks so any conflicting individuals do not work together or moving people onto different desks so they do not need to be near each other.

Finally, it may be necessary to take some more drastic actions such as removing constant offenders from the team or, it is it particularly severe, taking disciplinary action

- However, at all times, the Steering Committee, Sponsor and other relevant Senior Management must be kept updated regarding any issues and the actions being progressed to address them.

Key Takeaways

- If any human-related aspect issues are noticed then they need to be addressed immediately otherwise it will (a) cause issues with the change and (b) be very uncomfortable for the staff impacted.

- Therefore the Change Manager will need to ensure they are aware of any problems so the cause can be identified and the problems resolved.

- At all times, the Steering Committee, Sponsor and other relevant Senior Management need to be kept updated.

6.18 Remember that all changes will have issues and problems

Regardless of the amount of work performed and/or the skill of the Change Team, things will go wrong. This is because change is such a complex phenomenon. Therefore, stakeholders need to understand this and be taken along the journey. Remember most people are generally resistant to any type of change

The following diagram provides an interesting overview of the human reaction to change.

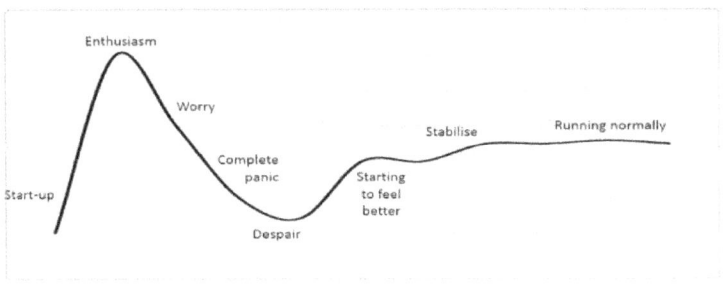

After the change started, there was a large amount of enthusiasm. Some problems were encountered which caused worry, panic and then despair. Once these issues were resolved, things got better, stabilised and the implementation started to run normally.

Therefore, all stakeholders need to be aware of this and understand problems do happen.

If some stakeholders are not aware of this then the Change Manager and Sponsor need to work with them to ensure they understand this. This awareness can be socialised by (a) ensuring all stakeholders understand the issues around budgets, scope, timelines, etc. and (b) they are constantly updated on progress via either the normal reporting or via one-off reports such as a special meeting, an email or ad-hoc update.

Key Takeaways

- Change is a complex subject and despite having the best plans in place there will be problems.

- Therefore, to manage expectations, all senior management must be aware of this.

6.19 Is the change experiencing scope creep?

One of the key challenges of implementing change successfully is the effective management of scope (or as it is sometimes called "scope creep"). This covers where items are both added or removed from the scope of the change but without any real control to ensure that their impact is assessed and often without senior stakeholders being aware of the amendments or having the opportunity to either approve or reject them,

All changes to scope (regardless of how small) will impact deliverables, timelines, and costs and therefore could ultimately impact whether a change is successful or not. There is a long list of changes that have struggled or even failed due to poor management of scope.

For all big changes to scope (such as a major change in requirements or a major milestone delay) then these should go through the formal change control process which is mentioned in section 5.18 earlier). If this is not happening then this is a massive issue and it is important that the Change Manager, Sponsor and Steering Committee address this immediately.

However, most of the "scope creep" challenges tend to relate to smaller changes that are not processed through the change Control process. (For example, making a small change to a technology requirement or adding a feature to a new product). This is because the scope changes are seen as small and irrelevant and/or that the change Control process is burdensome, bureaucratic and overkill. However, this means that the wider impact of the scope changes to cost, timelines, etc. are not known and also senior stakeholders are not aware of them nor have they approved them.

One could argue that individually these 'scope creep' items do not impact wider change because they are so small, but if a number of these small items happen then collectively they could materially impact the change at a holistic level. For example, the deliverables could be impacted, timelines can be missed, costs could overrun, etc.

This means, regardless of size, all alternations to scope must be processed through the change control process to ensure they impacted assessed, reviewed, approved or rejected by the relevant senior stakeholders. (To avoid the overheads of creating change Control requests for each separate smaller change then it is not uncommon for several smaller changes to be batched together onto a single change Control request).

Remember, the purpose of the change control process is not so much about the change itself but it is to ensure there is sufficient controls are in place to make sure that all change requests are fully assessed so that the relevant senior stakeholders can decide whether to approve or reject them.

Key Takeaways

- One of the key causes for change problems or failures is scope creep.

- Therefore organisations and Change Teams need to ensure that all scope changes (without fail) are processed through the change Control process.

- This will ensure that there is a sufficient process in place to make sure any requests are fully assessed so that the relevant senior stakeholders can decide whether to approve or reject them.

6.20 How paranoid is the Change Team about issues and problems?

As one will have noticed or learnt from this book, change is a complex process with a large number of unknowns, a constant altering set of issues/problems, a long list of tasks, a complex set of dependencies plus many other items.

Change is also impacted by adverse factors outside the control of the immediate Change Team such as regulatory or political changes.

Therefore, there is a real risk that things could change without the Change Team knowing or realising. This could then cause the change to fail or, at best, experience several implementation problems.

This means the Change Manager (and the Change Team in general) need to be very paranoid about things going wrong. This could cover many areas such as items being missed items, tasks being overlooked, tasks running late, tasks not starting on time, people not being aware of what they need to, etc.

To mitigate this, the Change Manager will need to constantly review all aspects of the change to look for issues, problems, items that have been forgotten, etc. The Change Manager should also encourage team members to raise issues even if they think they are red herrings.

Remember, it is much better to raise an issue and waste thirty minutes now on a non-issue than not to raise now that eventually transforms into a major problem that could cost a large amount of time and money to fix later.

Therefore, to implement successful change, it helps to be very paranoid about things going wrong.

Key Takeaways

- Change is complex and things can alter without the Change Team being aware of them. This can cause problems with implementation.

- This means the Change Manager (and team) need to be very paranoid about things going wrong and changing.

- They need to constantly re-review the change regularly to trap any problems.

- Remember only the paranoid deliver change

6.21 Are staff comfortable raising issues and/or problems without the threat of repercussions from management or other colleges?

This question is linked closely with 6.10 (Identifying and managing resistance), 6.17 (Managing human aspects), 6.18 (Understanding that all changes have issues) and 6.20 (Being paranoid about change). There is some overlap and duplication across these items and this question but this is a key point and it is important that is it raised as a separate question.

In some organisations whose culture is 'tough' and 'alpha male', the raising of issues or making mistakes is often seen as a weakness. (These organisations are often run along the lines of "do not bring me problems, only bring me solutions"). These perceived weaknesses can result in punishments from the organisations. These punishments can either be hidden or invisible, such as being ignored or shunned, passed over for promotion for no apparent reason or being perceived as weak or poor at your job. Punishment can also be very visible such as poor performance appraisals or even in some cases disciplinary action. Also, they could result in humiliation or abuse in front of others such as being criticised in front of others, humiliated in meetings or being sent abusive emails.

However, this behaviour does cause problems when implementing change. This is because people will be frightened to raise issues which means issues will be hidden and will therefore fester into something nasty. This could result in either change problems or even change failure.

Unfortunately, for a Change Manager, this is a hard situation to manage.

One option is to raise the issue with the Sponsor and or Steering Committee. But if this culture is organisational wide, these people could be part of the problem. It could make things worse by raising it, because the Change Manager may then be perceived as a trouble maker and/or weak at their job.

The only real way is for the Change Manager to work with the change team members on an individual basis to try and understand and tease out 'hidden' issues and problems.

Similar to the points made in section 6.10 earlier, people need a safe space to raise and discuss issues. Remember if people feel threatened, scared or worried about being punished or persecuted then they will not raise any problems and they will continue to fester and cause problems. It is much better to hold these types of discussions on a 1-2-1 basis. This can either be face-to-face, over the telephone or via video conference. Remember, people are much more open on a one to one basis. This 1-2-1 basis allows the Change Manager to ask deeper questions much more tactically regarding the points being raised. The Change Manager will need good soft and interpersonal skills so they can ask the correct questions which allow the required information to be obtained without making people feel threatened and/or nervous.

Also is important to remember any points raised remain anonymous. Remember if people feel worried that a problem or a mistake could be traced back to them (especially if they're going to feel blamed or punished) then they will not raise them.

Unfortunately, because all the issues that have been raised are anonymous then a very careful approach needs to be followed regarding how to raise and manage them (but ensuring the people who raise the problems are kept anonymous) across the wider change team. There are two main options.

- The first option is for the Change Manager to raise them by asking 'dumb questions' at (say) a team meeting. For example, do we think that XYZ is an issue? Have we covered ABC? Etc. By raising this then it allows the Change Manager to bring people into the conversation, determine whether it is a real issue, discuss the impact and agree on a way or plan forward.

- The second option is for the Change Manager to raise the issue by saying they have experienced similar problems on previous changes or at previous organisations. For example "when I worked on Change XYZ at Organisation ABC, we had this issue which caused all sorts of problems - do we feel that this could be a problem on this change?" This will allow the Change Manager to bring people into the conversation, determine whether it is a real issue or not, discuss the impact and agree on a way or plan forward.

The benefit of this approach here is that the issue is raised, discussed and an approach is agreed to address it but the people who raise the issue are protected.

Key Takeaways

- It is important the Change Team members (and other key staff) feel comfortable to raise issues and problems without fear of punishment.

- Otherwise, problems will not be addressed which could impact whether the Change is successful or not.

- If the Change Manager feels that people are uncomfortable about raising issues then they need to work with the impacted individuals on a 1-2-1 basis to (a) allow them to raise problems anonymously so (b) they can be addressed and managed.

6.22 Is the Change Team being appreciated for their work and efforts?

(This question regarding appreciating people for their efforts is a common thread throughout the different stages of implementing change. This means that it appears a few times in this book. This has created some duplication but because this is an important point, then it is justified).

There is a tendency when implementing change to focus on the problems encountered and not to look at what has good well or thank people for their efforts and hard work.

As noted several times earlier, implementing change is stressful, requires people to work long hours and can be demotivating if problems are being constantly discovered. Therefore it is important for the Sponsor, Change Manager, Steering Committee members and other senior managers to appreciate the efforts and achievements of the Change Team. For example, completing a phase of the change or agreeing on commercial terms with a new supplier.

It makes the team feel appreciated and it also motivates them for the future. It is amazing the positive impact that a simple "thank you" or "well done" will have especially if it is unexpected and is received from a senior member of management. Therefore the Sponsor, Change Manager, Steering Committee members and other senior managers should be aware of the efforts of the Change Team and the achievements and send out "thank you" or "well done" messages to the relevant team members.

Also, another significant way to provide a reward is to review the positive team member's performance and make this known to their managers. Changes are often not part of the employee's day job and there could be resentment on undertaking additional project tasks which are not going to impact the employees' reviews and appraisals.

Key Takeaways

- Changes can be stressful especially if team members are working long hours and/or there is a constant wave of issues.

- The senior stakeholders need to appreciate the efforts and achievements of the Change Team.

- It makes the team feel appreciated and it also motivates them for the future.

- Therefore senior stakeholders should be aware of the efforts of the Change Team and the achievements and send out "thank you" or "well done" messages to the relevant team members as appropriate.

- Finally, it is a good idea to tell the manager of Change Team members that they have performed a good job.

6.23 Remember to keep checking whether the triggers, business case, benefits, etc. are still valid?

Even the simplest change will take some time to implement and during this implementation period, two things could happen.

Firstly, the external market dynamics could change. This could be due to many different reasons such as new competition, customer requirements changing, regulations changing, etc. If this happens then it could mean that the triggers for the change, its business case, the requirements, etc. could now be invalid which, in turn, could mean, the change is now not needed or the change needs to be rethought. There is a long list of changes that have been implemented where the reason or the need for change has either gone away or has changed considerably. If this happens then the change will be a failure.

Secondly, the organisation could change itself. Again this could be for several reasons. For example, they have changed their market focus, they are looking at different client segments, they are now focused on reducing costs as opposed to increasing profits, etc. Therefore, if this happens, then it means that change is being implemented for an 'out of date' strategy as opposed to the current 'up to date' strategy. The result is that the change could be invalid and therefore suspect to failure. This means that if an organisation alters their strategy then they need to review all changes in progress to ensure they are either updated to tie in with the new strategy or terminated completely

Therefore, it is important to constantly review all changes in progress to ensure their triggers for change, business cases, benefits, etc. are still valid. It is very possible that during the implementation of a change, there could be shifts in the external environment or the organisation alters itself that could invalidate the triggers, business case, etc. If so either the change needs to be updated to reflect this or terminated. Otherwise, the change will be a failure.

Key Takeaways

- It is important to constantly review all changes in progress to ensure their triggers for change, business cases, etc. are still valid.

- It is possible that during the implementation of a change, there could be alternations in the external environment or the organisation alters itself that could invalidate the triggers, business case, etc.

- If so either the change needs to be updated to reflect this or terminated. Otherwise, the change will be a failure.

7 Has sufficient preparation been performed for the go-live transition?

"Good luck is a residue of preparation"
- Jack Youngblood

7.1 Introduction

As one may have gathered from earlier parts of this book, successful change relies on ensuring the organisation has the skills and capability to make the change, the change is pre-planned and is implemented proactive and with suitable controls. However, it is also important to spend sufficient time and thought on the go-live or transition event.

Therefore this means these events need to be thoroughly prepared for. This covers ensuring there is ownership of the change post-go-live, sufficient training and awareness have been completed plus that any transition checklist has been completed and tested thoroughly.

It would be a real shame to perform all the earlier parts of the change perfectly but slip up on this final part. It would mean the change would be unsuccessful. Some transition events can be very complex, large, and risky and could take several weeks to fully implement which can mean that transition activities could be viewed as separate changes in their own right.

This section lists several questions that organisations should check when they are preparing to transition a change into the live world. Each question focused on a particular challenge that could cause problems and then offers some guidance on how these areas can be addressed.

7.2 Has everything been delivered that is needed for transition? (And what are the impacts of any gaps)

Despite the best efforts of the Change Team and other related stakeholders, not everything will be ready at the transition date. This could be due to many reasons.

One good reason there is a non-movable go-live date, and there is not sufficient time to deliver everything before this date. This means it is necessary to go live with the change by this non-movable date and then address any gaps afterwards. A good example of this was BREXIT where there was an unmovable end-2020 date where the UK left the EU, and organisations had to ensure they had done the minimum amount of change required to comply with this and then address any other items during 2021 and later.

Alternately, there could be overruns on tasks (which means deliverables are going to be missed) but the Steering Committee may just want to get the change live as quickly as possible to ensure they start to receive the benefits of the change as opposed to the perception of the change running on and on.

Also, there could be a market need where there is a need to launch a product to keep up with market demands and competition. The Steering Committee and other senior management may decide to launch partially to meet this need and address any gaps issues at a later date.

There are also many other examples.

While this can be frustrating annoying, it is a part of managing and implementing successful change and these situations need to be managed appropriately. If they are not managed then it can result in confusion, frustration, errors, and even possible change failure. This situation can be managed in five parts.

- The first task is to understand what has not been delivered. For example, are product or service features missing? Is technology functionality missing? Are there legal gaps? Are the staffing issues? etc.

- Once this list of issues has or gaps has been created, then the organisation needs to understand what the impact of these gaps are. For example, is there key functionality missing? Are there gaps in the service offering which could impact customers? Will there be operating cost increases? Will the risk profile of the organisation increase in an uncomfortable way? Would the gaps result in accounting errors? Will the gaps result in regulatory breaches? etc.

- For each of the delivery gaps then interim solutions need to be implemented to manage these gaps when the change transitions into the live environment. These solutions can range greatly. For example, extra people can be employed to cover any extra manual processes required, tactical technology solutions (such as Spreadsheets) can be used, etc.

- Once interim solutions are designed then the Change needs to determine how these gaps can be 'plugged' long term and permanent. Again there are many different ways that this can be addressed.

    One common option is to have a second phase of the change initiative, which is in effect is extending the Change initiative to complete these remaining issues. However, the Sponsor, Steering Committee and senior management may not want to do this because it will increase costs and tie up critical staff which could be employed more beneficially on other initiatives.

Another common alternative, is that gaps are fixed in the Post Transition Support, Warranty or Hypercare activity (see Section 9).

Finally, it is not that uncommon for these gaps to be dropped completely. Again his could be various reasons for this. The Steering Committee could decide after all that these omissions are not that important, or the Steering Committee just want to close the change and move on to other important and pressing initiatives. However, if these are dropped then all stakeholders need to clearly understand what the long term implications are because it could result in challenges for the day-to-day running of the operations, services, products, etc.

- Finally, it is essential to ensure that all relevant stakeholders (such as the Sponsor, the Steering Committee, other senior management, customers, suppliers, regulators, etc.) are aware of these gaps in delivery, the immediate impact when the change transitions into live, how these gaps will be managed in the interim and how they will be fixed long term. Also, as part of this communication, this group of stakeholders will need to receive regular updates as and when these gaps are 'plugged'

Key Takeaways

- Despite the best efforts of the Change Team and other related stakeholders, not everything will be ready at the transition date.

- While this can be frustrating annoying, it is a part of managing and implementing successful change and these situations need to be managed appropriately. If they are not managed then it can result in confusion, frustration, errors, and even possible change failure.

- Therefore all stakeholders must be aware of these gaps in delivery, the immediate impact when the change transitions into live, how these gaps will be managed in the interim and how they will be fixed long term.

7.3 Is everything that needs to be transitioned into live working as planned?

In a similar vein to section 7.2 above, it is important to check that everything that has been delivered and is going to be deployed works as designed. In other words, is it 'fit for purpose' or does it contain defects?

Transitioning a change into production with defects will cause problems and could result in a change failure. (These defects could cover many areas such as are all processes working? Are all staff fully trained? Does all the technology work? Are the legal arrangements fully correct? Has everything been fully tested? Have all sign-offs been completed? Etc.).

In an ideal world, everything should be working perfectly before going live. However, the reality is that this is not always possible. For example, there may be a change that needs to go live by a certain date (say due to a legislation change) and the implications of missing this date could be greater than going live with a solution that has defects.

This means that it is a case of having a clear understanding of any (a) what the full list of defects and their impact and any mitigations are so (b) it will allow the Sponsor, Steering

Committee and other Senior Management can take an informed and proactive decision on whether to transition the change into production or wait until a later date.

While it is likely the Change Team will have a list of defects created as part of the normal implementation effort, there is always a risk that there could be unknown defects or defects that have slipped through any governance. (Again this is especially true for complex changes).

Therefore, if there is any doubt whatsoever, then is a good idea to perform a final review of everything that has been performed to ensure nothing has been missed. This will involve speaking in depth with the change team, business users, suppliers, customers and other key stakeholders to ask them are they aware of anything due to be transitioned into production that may not be working as designed. (Remember section 6.20 about being paranoid).

Once this list of defects has been created then the organisation needs to understand what their impact is? For example, will they cause key functionality to fail? How will they impact customers? Will they cause a health-and-safety risk? Etc.

After this, the Change Team needs to design 'stop gap' mitigations to manage these defects when the change transitions into the live environment. For example, do extra people need to be employed to cover missing functionality? Are spreadsheets required to cover defects in technology? Etc.

Once these 'stop gap' mitigations are designed then the Change Teams needs to determine how these defects can be fixed in the long term. Again (similar to section 7.2 above), there are many different ways that this can be addressed.

- One option is to have a second phase of the change, which is in effect is extending the Change initiative to fix the defects.

- Another common alternative, is that gaps are fixed in the Post Transition Support, Warranty or Hypercare activity (see Section 9).

- A final option is that it is agreed that the business can live with these defects and no plans are made to fix them. This could be for many reasons. The Steering Committee could decide after all that these defects are not that important, or the Steering Committee just want to close the change and move on to other important and pressing initiatives.

Once the analysis of the list of defects, their impacts, their mitigations and long-term fixes are completed then it will allow the Sponsor, Steering Committee and other impacted senior management can take an informed and proactive decision on whether to transition the change into production.

They may decide to wait until all the defects (or at least the material ones) are addressed. The advantages of this approach are that it reduces the risk of problems being caused by these defects, but it would both (a) delay the change going live with the associated business benefits and (b) incur extra costs and distractions with the change running longer.

Although it may be necessary to go to live with a change with these defects fully addressed. For example, there may be a hard go-live date that must be met. The advantage of this is that the change goes live with associated benefits, but this is counterbalanced by the risk that there of these defects causing issues post-transition

Key Takeaways

- It is important to have a clear understanding that everything due to be transitioned into the production environment is working as planned.

- This understanding of defects will allow (a) their impact to be assessed (b) any mitigations to be designed (c) long term fix plan to be devised so (c) the Sponsor, Steering Committee and other Senior Management can take an informed and proactive decision on whether to transition the change into production or wait until a later date.

- Transitioning a change into production with unknown or unmanaged defects will cause problems and could result in a change failure.

7.4 Has a Transition Coordinator been nominated?

Even the simplest of transitions are complex. They always involve a large number of tasks to be completed, many issues to manage, many communications to be performed, the review of control points, managing any control meetings, tracking the point of no return (see 7.9), etc.

Therefore, somebody must be nominated to be the Transition Coordinator. The person's responsibilities are ensuring (a) all the pre-transition work is completed (such as planning, testing, etc.) (b) the transition activity and, if necessary, roll-back activity is completed and (c) all post-transition activity is managed such as ensuring any problems or issues raised are managed to a close.

This means it is important this role is filled as early as possible.

This person will need to report to either the Change Manager (as the person responsible for delivering the change at the 'on the ground' level) or report to the Steer Committee or Sponsor. The Transition Coordinator will need to have the authority to make the transition happen.

Without this role in place, then there is a real risk that the transition will not be coordinated which effectively could mean the transition (or rollback) is not completed. This will no doubt mean the transition and wider change will fail but it could also impact the wider business operation if the transition or rollback causes issues.

Sometimes the Change Manager will do the Transition Co-coordinator role themselves because it will reduce complexity and duplication. The Change Manager is often a good fit because they will know about the change as well as all the elements within it. However, if the Change Manager is still working on the actual implementation then they could become overloaded with the volume of work.

Similarly, some (again typically larger) organisations have specialist Transition Coordinators in their employment. These are people with experience in running transitions. Although they will need to be brought up to speed on the change and to ensure that they understand their roles and responsibilities with the Change Manager.

Similarly, some (again larger) organisations may use different (sub) Transition Coordinators to work in different areas or disciplines. For example, a specialist coordinator will be employed to look after the technology migrations, another could be deployed to ensure any external communication is performed, another could oversee post-implementation support etc. If this does happen then an overall Transition Coordinator is still required and this person will still have overall responsibility and accountability for ensuring the transition happens. Any of these (sub) Transition Co-ordinators will still need to report to this overall Transition Co-ordinator.

The key point to remember is that a single person (i.e. Transition Coordinator) needs to be employed and be accountable to the Steering Committee and Sponsor to ensure the transition is completed fully. If this person is not in place then the Transition could fail which will cause issues with the change and the wider organisation.

Key Takeaways

- To ensure a transition (and roll back if required) is completed successfully then a single person needs to be employed and be accountable to the Steering Committee and Sponsor to ensure the transition is completed

- This person is called the Transition Coordinator and their role covers are ensuring (a) all the pre-transition work is completed (such as planning, testing, etc.) (b) actual transition activity and, if necessary, roll-back activity is completed and (c) all post-transition activity is managed such as ensuring any problems or issues raised are managed to a close.

- This role should be filled as early as possible.

- If this person is not in place then the Transition could fail which will cause issues with the change and the wider organisation. (Although sometimes the Change Manager will perform this role).

- It may be necessary to use several different (sub) Transitions Coordinators to focus on specific areas and disciplines but these people will need to report to the main Transition Coordinator to ensure there is control, focus and accountability.

7.5 Has the transition approach been agreed upon?

At the start of the change (see Section 5.12 earlier), it is suggested that it would be worthwhile having some type of idea of how the change will transition into the live environment. (To recap, the actual transition could cover many areas such as moving into new offices, changing business processes, launching new products, upgrading technology, moving staff to new roles, etc.)

This would help with planning especially regarding who needs to be involved, the governance structure, workstream structure, costs etc. It would also help set expectations with stakeholders (such as the Sponsor, Steering Committee, suppliers, customers and even regulators) on how the transition would look and allow them to raise issues when everything was still very much at the planning or thinking stage as opposed to now when work on the transitions is starting properly.

To recap, there are several different types of transitions.

- One is the traditional big bang approach where the entire change transitions in the live environment at once. For example, upgrading a new piece of software or technology. The transition period is often very short (say an evening or a weekend) but there is a large amount of risk trying to perform all the transition activities at once.

- However, it is becoming more and more common to use phased transitions. This reduces the risk of a "big bang" but does increase the length of the transition. For example, using a new product launch. An initial test launch could be initially performed with a target customer base with the focus on testing that the product and the support processes work. If there are issues then they can be addressed before any later phases.

- Also, phased approaches are often necessary due to a lack of time to complete the full transition. For example, the author once worked on a large outsourcing change. There were a large number of business activities that had to be transitioned from the in-house team to the outsourcing supplier, and there was not enough time to perform them over a weekend (even a bank holiday weekend). This meant the transition was split over several weekends spread over several months. This increased the length and complexity of the migration but avoided a risky "big bang" approach.

Nevertheless, during the implementation of the change, the previously thought approach may well have changed for a wide range of very plausible and valid reasons. For example, the change is more complex or the requirements have altered which means a different transition approach is required.

However at this stage of the change (i.e. pre-transition planning), then it is essential that the approach has been confirmed and agreed with required stakeholders (such as the Sponsor, the Steering Committee and other key stakeholders such as customers and suppliers).

If there is still any uncertainty or lack of agreement on how the transition should be structured then this is a major issue and needs to be addressed by the Change Team and wider stakeholders immediately. No transition planning (yet along with the actual transition itself) should start until an approach is crystal clear and agreed with all required stakeholders. Otherwise, not only with the change probably fail, but a failed or poorly thought through transitions could materially impact all aspects of the business.

Key Takeaways

- By this stage of the change (i.e. pre-transition planning) then it is essential that the approach has been confirmed and agreed upon with required stakeholders

- If there is still any uncertainty or lack of agreement then this is a major issue and needs to be addressed by the Change Team and wider stakeholders immediately.

- No transition planning (let alone the actual transition itself) should start until an approach is crystal clear and agreed with all required stakeholders.

- Otherwise, not only with the change probably fail, but a failed or poorly thought through transitions could materially impact all aspects of the business.

7.6 Is everybody aware that the transition is going to take place?

It is important that all, directly and indirectly, stakeholders are aware that the transition is taking place. This should be part of the normal communications approaches discussed earlier in this book. But it is still worth mentioning here due to its importance.

Those within the Change Team or who are directly impacted by the change should know this through their involvement with the change. However, stakeholders who are not directly involved in the change could have no idea that the change is in progress and that a transition is being planned. This could be a problem because certain complex transitions could result in business functions not being available for long periods. For example, websites being unavailable for a full weekend or certain business functions closing early to allow the transition to start.

A lack of awareness may not cause the transition and change to fail specifically but it could cause issues with other teams, customers and suppliers which could be embarrassing and take the 'shine' of a successful implementation.

Therefore all areas (covering internal teams as well as suppliers and customers) must be aware that the transition is taking place. There are many different ways this awareness can be spread but the most effective method is via a regular set of planned communications. Namely:

- The Sponsor (or senior member of management) will send regular communications (normally emails) to all stakeholders that could be impacted. It will need to outline what the change is, what services (such as websites) could be unavailable during the transition and who should be contacted if there are any questions.

- The first message would typically be many weeks before the transition event to (a) ensure all people are aware of it and (b) give them sufficient time to make other arrangements if services are not available.

- Any further communications would be in the weeks or days before the transition event to (a) ensure everybody is aware and has not missed or forgotten the earlier communications and (b) allow them to raise any further questions or queries.

Key Takeaways

- Transitions events may need certain services to be temporality closed (such as losing a website for a weekend or not being able to trade in the evenings).

- All stakeholders either within or external to the organisation must be aware of any possible outages because (a) it will cause material problems and (b) they will need to make temporary arrangements

- This means that there needs to be a structured communication process to ensure all relevant people are made aware with sufficient notice.

7.7 Is there clear ownership of the change before it is transitioned into live?

The ownership of the change when it goes live should have been addressed earlier in the change but is always a good idea to double-check.

Allocating ownership can be surprisingly challenging. If the change is implementing something completely new then there may not be a natural owner. Also, there could be organisational politics in place which teams use to stop them from owning the change.

Changes that do not have a clear owner when they go live tend to struggle. This is because the Change Team continue to own the new processes or ownership is given to somebody at short notice which means they did not have sufficient time to prepare to take on the change.

If there is no owner before go-live then this should be escalated to the Sponsor and Steering Committee immediately for resolution. No change should transition into live unless there is a clear owner.

Key Takeaways

- All changes must have a pre-agreed owner before they go live

- If there is no owner before go-live then this should be escalated to the Sponsor and Steering Committee immediately for resolution.

- No change should transition into live unless there is a clear owner.

7.8 Has sufficient training been performed before go-live?

All changes require some sort of process change or alternation. For example, there could be new technology screens, new processes that need following, new reports that will be produced etc. These process changes could be spread across a variety of organisations. For example, the organisation making the change as well as its suppliers and customers.

Therefore, for a change to be successful then all staff must be trained in these changes and know how to use them when everything goes live. If they are not trained then it will cause problems and the change will not be successful. Also, the training will ensure that all procedures, processes and policies are updated accordingly.

There are various ways that training can be performed; namely:

- There is the traditional classroom where training is performed either on a face to face basis or via video conference. This is suitable if there is a low number of people attending but if the audience is large or spread across many locations or time zones then this approach will not work.

- Training can also be performed by reading documentation. The Change Team could produce process flows, swim lane diagrams, user manuals, hints-and-tips sheets and lists of frequently asked questions. While this is very useful, this documentation is best to support training performed using a different method. For example, these documents could be hand-outs at the end of classroom training sessions.

- Another alternative that is becoming increasingly popular is video recordings. The training courses are pre-recorded and staff view them at leisure (but obviously before the change goes live).

- A further approach that is also becoming more common is interactive training. This is similar to video recordings where the user will follow a series of pre-recorded videos and slides but there will be many questions asked during the training which need to be answered correctly to allow the person to proceed. This will ensure that the staff member is learning what is being trained.

One of the biggest challenges regarding training is ensuring the people attending the training have understood and learnt what is changing. This is especially important where change impacts some series such as dangerous machinery or regulatory areas. Therefore some organisations are asking their staff to complete an end-of-training test to prove that they have understood the training. If they fail the test then they need to redo the training until they pass. Escalations will be in place for constant failures or for not doing the training at all.

Key Takeaways

- All changes require some sort of process change or alternation.

- Therefore, for a change to be successful then all staff (cover internal teams, suppliers and customers) must be trained in these changes and know how to use them when everything goes live.

- This will ensure that all processes, policies and procedures are updated.

- If they are not trained then it will cause problems and the change will not be successful.

7.9 Is there a robust transition plan in place?

It is essential that the transition event is planned in as much detail as possible otherwise there will be problems

Poor transition management is a major reason for change failure. It would be a real shame to perform all the earlier parts of the change perfectly but slip up on this final part. The Transition Coordinator should be responsible for creating this plan (although they will need help from the rest of the Change Team). If the Transition Coordinator and/or Change Manager is encountering any issues with collating the plan then they must be escalated to the Sponsor, Steering Committee and other senior management.

The transition contains many parts namely some type of a list of the tasks to complete the transition, the required people to perform the work and sufficient controls and checks. Namely:

A list of transition tasks needs to be created

Each go-live event will require a set of tasks to be completed. This range of tasks can cover many areas such as technology changes, data migration, writing to clients plus many more. These activities will be spread over some time. For example, for simple changes (say covering 20 to 30 tasks) then the transition could be competing with a couple of hours or an evening. But for a more complex transition, there could be several thousand tasks that could take a full weekend or even longer. For this reason, it is not unusual for complex transitions to be scheduled over bank holiday weekends because it provides more time to implement and if required rollback.

This list of tasks needs to be converted into a full transition plan and resource list

Once the list of tasks is understood then they need to be converted into a detailed Transition Plan or Checklist which will list all the tasks that need to be completed, their order, their dependencies, when they need to be completed and who will need to perform the work (such as internal, suppliers, customers, regulators and many others. The owners of these tasks will need to agree to own them.

Remember that some tasks may be done outside working hours

When the plan is drafted (or at least when the first draft is completed), it will be a good idea to review when certain activities need to be done. If they need to be done out of hours or during unsociable hours then this may mean people may need to work from home or arrangements may be made to allow them to travel into the office or stay in hotels overnight.

Think about what could go wrong and include fall-back or contingency plans

There is a long list of problems that could be encountered and it is important as many of these are investigated at this planning stage so contingency or fall-back plans can be devised. For example, if people need to travel into the office then it may be necessary to ensure either there is a taxi firm available in case public transport is not available or they can access remotely from home. Likewise, if the transition requires a large number of data files to be moved then ensure there is different fall-back options is cause the preferred method does not work (such as using disks or emails).

The transition plan should have several control points to provide early warning of issues

To ensure the transition is proceeding to plan, then several control points need to be included. These control points will typically be time checks to verify whether tasks are running behind and will therefore act as an early indicator of possible problems. For example, if a certain task has not been done by a certain time then a warning can be raised.

These controls points should be supported by control meetings where key stakeholders (such as the Change Team, Change Manager, Sponsor, Steering Committee and even possibly representatives from key suppliers and customers). At the meetings, the progress of the transition will be reviewed to see if there are any issues or whether remediation is required.

The transition plan should include the point of no return

It will also be useful to indicate or include what the points of no return are. This is the latest time that any rollback plan can be started to ensure that all rollback activity is completed in time to minimise any impact generally across the organisation. For example, if it takes four hours to roll back then it would be advisable to have the point of no return say six hours before the start of business which will cover the four hours to complete the roll-back plus two extra hours contingency.

Key Takeaways

- A transition event must be planned in as much detail as possible otherwise there will be problems

- This plan should be driven by the Transition Coordinator.

- Poor transition management is a reason for change failure. It would be a real shame to perform all the earlier parts of the change perfectly but slip up on this final part

- The transition plan contains many parts namely some type of a list of the tasks to complete the transition, the required people to perform the work and sufficient controls and checks

- It is important to understand the "Point of no return". This is the latest time that any rollback plan can be started to ensure that all rollback activity is completed in time to minimise any impact generally across the organisation.

- It is also important to think about what things could go wrong and ensure there are fall-back or contingency plans in place.

- If the Change Manager is encountering any issues with collating the plan then they must be escalated to the Sponsor, Steering Committee and other senior management.

7.10 Is there a sufficient rollback plan in place?

Similarly to the transition plan detailed above it is important a robust rollback plan is created in case there are issues with running the transition. Depending on the transitions and possible problems then there could be different rollback plans contingent on different failures. These rollback plans will need to follow the same disciplines (noted in 7.7 above) such as a list of the tasks to complete the roll-back, the required people to perform the work, sufficient controls and checks, etc. except that everything is in reverse.

A fully working roll-back plan must be in place. Imagine the disastrous situation if change started to transition into live but failed and it was not possible to roll back to the original position?

This could cause a business to fail and material consequences to its clients, suppliers and the general marketplace. Also, having a working roll-back plan provides confidence to all stakeholders that the transition can be reversed in the event of problems.

The Transition Coordinator should be responsible for creating this roll-back plan (although they will need help from the rest of the Change Team). If the Transition Coordinator and/or Change Manager is encountering any issues with collating the plan then they must be escalated to the Sponsor, Steering Committee and other senior management.

Furthermore, it is also key to understand how long the rollback takes because it will need to inform the "point of no return" in the main transition plan (see section 7.9). Repeating the example from above in section 7.9, if it takes four hours to roll back then it would be advisable to have the point of no return say six hours before the start of business. This will cover four hours to complete the roll-back plus two extra hours contingency.

Key Takeaways

- All transition events and plans must be accompanied by a set of roll-back plans to cover all the types of problems that could be encountered.

- This plan must exist so that any transition can be rolled back in the event of problems. Imagine the disastrous situation if change started to transition into live but failed and it was not possible to roll back to the original position?

- The Transition Manager should be responsible for completing the roll-back plan.

- The roll-back plan contains many parts namely some type of a list of the tasks to complete the transition, the required people to perform the work and sufficient controls and checks

- If the Change Manager is encountering any issues with collating the roll-back plan then they must be escalated to the Sponsor, Steering Committee and other senior management.

7.11 Have both the transition and rollback plans been tested (both separately and together)?

Both the transition and roll-back plans must be tested thoroughly. This is to ensure that the tasks are correct, the dependencies are valid, the control points work as planned, all timings are correct, people know what they need to do and to generally provide confidence that the plans are fit-for-purpose.

It is pointless creating a plan and not test it because it will create a false sense of security.

If they are not tested then there is no guarantee that the plan works which could be disastrous when trying either run the transition or the roll-back. This could cause an organisation to fail with nasty consequences to its clients, suppliers and the general marketplace.

There are different ways the plans can be tested.

- At the simplest level, there could be a simple desk walkthrough, where everybody sits around the desk and steps through the plan in a meeting. No actual activity is done and the focus is on ensuring that the relevant tasks and dependencies are in place. A desk walkthrough is often a good first test of a plan.

- A second option is to perform a dry run. This is where the Change Team run through the plan from the start to the end but typically during normal working hours. The actual activities are performed so it is good for checking that the plan works with the correct tasks, dependences and people doing the work. However, a dry run is not always good for testing timings and trying to replicate the challenges of performing the plan over weekends, evenings or at other unsocial times

- The third (and probably the best option) is to perform a full dress rehearsal. This is where the Change Team test the plan in a situation that replicates as much as possible that will happen when the plans are executed properly. For example, all tasks are followed, the people who will do the work will do the work, people will work the required unsocial hours, people may need to stay in hotels, and the control points are followed etc. A successful dress rehearsal will provide a large amount of confidence that the plans are fit-for-purpose.

The individual transition and roll-back plans need to be tested separately but it is also advisable to test them together. This is to ensure that the roll-back plans devised can resolve a failed transition. A typical flow would be to (a) run the transition fully (b) roll it back and then (c) re-run the transition. Another flow could be to (a) run the transition but ensure it fails in some way (b) roll it back and then (c) re-run the transition

The more complex and/or business-critical the transition is then the more testing is required. It is not uncommon for some transitions and roll-backs to perform several dry-runs, desk walkthroughs and dress rehearsals.

The Transition Coordinator should be responsible for ensuring all the required testing is completed. If the Transition Coordinator and/or Change Manager is encountering any issues with collating the plan then they must be escalated to the Sponsor, Steering Committee and other senior management.

Key Takeaways

- All transition and roll-back plans need to be tested thoroughly both separately and together.

- This testing is required to ensure that the plans are fit-for-purpose.

- The Transition Coordinator should ensure the testing is completed.

- It would be extremely risky to proceed with any type of transition without a set of fully and thoroughly tested transition and rollback plans. This is because there would be

- If the Change Manager is encountering any issues with collating the roll-back plan then they must be escalated to the Sponsor, Steering Committee and other senior management.

7.12 Is the Change Team being appreciated for their work and efforts?

(This question regarding appreciating people for their efforts is a common thread throughout the different stages of implementing change. This means that it appears a few times in this book. This has created some duplication but because this is an important point, then it is justified).

There is a tendency when preparing to transition a change in production to focus only on the problems encountered and not thank people for their efforts and hard work and for completing activities.

All aspects of implementing change can be stressful, require people to work long hours and can be demotivating if problems are being constantly discovered. Therefore it is important for the Sponsor, Change Manager, Steering Committee members and other senior managers to appreciate the efforts and achievements of the Change Team. For example, completing a phase of the change or agreeing on commercial terms with a new supplier

It makes the team feel appreciated and it also motivates them for the future. It is amazing the positive impact that a simple "thank you" or "well done" will have especially if it is unexpected and is received from a senior member of management.

Therefore the Sponsor, Change Manager, Steering Committee members and other senior managers should be aware of the efforts of the Change Team and the achievements and send out "thank you" or "well done" messages to the relevant team members.

Finally, another noticeable way to provide a reward is to review the positive team member's performance and make this known to their managers. Changes are often not part of the employee's day job and there could be resentment on undertaking additional project tasks which are not going to impact the employees' reviews and appraisals.

Key Takeaways

- Changes can be stressful especially if team members are working long hours and/or there is a constant wave of issues.

- The senior stakeholders need to appreciate the efforts and achievements of the Change Team.

- It makes the team feel appreciated and it also motivates them for the future.

- Therefore senior stakeholders should be aware of the efforts of the Change Team and the achievements and send out "thank you" or "well done" messages to the relevant team members as appropriate.

8 Care is still required during the actual transition event

"Any transition is easier if you believe in yourself and your talent"
- Priyanka Chopra

8.1 Introduction

Once all the pre-change work, the change execution activities and the transition/rollback planning is complete then the Change Team is now ready to run the transition into the live environment. Remember that a transition could be anything from a single "big bang" implementation to a series of smaller transitions that are spread over numerous weeks or sometimes even months.

However, despite all the preparation and testing work completed, executing any type of transition is still a challenging, stressful and testing time. This means it is important the Change Team (as well as the wider organisation) will need to follow the transition (and if necessary rollback) plans previously developed and tested. They should only diverge from them with real caution.

Although, having said this, all stakeholders need to be aware that problems and issues will happen regardless of the amount of preparation and testing performed. Some of the issues would be red-herrings and can be ignored but others could be real problems that need addressing the heat of the transition (or even rollback) event. Therefore any transition and roll-back plans must have sufficient controls included to track and review progress, problems and issues so that senior stakeholders (such as the Sponsor and/or Steering Committee) are aware of them just in case they need to make a major decision like approving a roll-back.

The world is littered with failed changes that did not follow the previously developed plans or did not have sufficient controls in place.

The structure of this section is based on a list of questions that organisations should be checking when they are transitioning a change into the live world. Each question focused on a particular problem that can hinder successful change and offers some guidance on how these areas can be addressed.

8.2 Issues and problems will happen so prepare for them and a cool head is needed to manage them

It is important to remember that go-live transitions (and if required rollbacks) can be stressful and tense situations. Apart from the pressure of performing the actual work, team members could be working long hours, fatigued, working weekends, up against time pressures, staying in hotels and working away from home.

These extra factors create something called 'stress fog'.

If problems appear then this 'stress fog' can alter the nature of these problems into something that is perceived to be either far more or even far less serious than it is. This means it is important that stakeholders fully understand the impact of problems so they can be managed accordingly. Apart from creating unhelpful and unnecessary alarm, it could result in poor decision making such as taking no action, taking unnecessary action which could cause others problems, deciding to roll back when it is not needed or even not rolling back when a rollback is required.

Therefore once problems are issues are discovered then they need careful analysis and management. It is best normally to allocate a single person (usually the Transition Co-ordinator) to own the management of any issues. They will need to work quickly and logically with the Change Team and any other stakeholders (such as subject-matter-experts) to understand clearly what the issue is, assess its impact on the overall transition/rollback, determine what actions (if any) are required, work with senior stakeholders (such as the Sponsor and Steering Committee) do agree what actions are necessary and then ensure these actions are implemented so the issue can be addressed and then closed. The type of actions that could be followed out can cover a wide range of many areas; for example carrying on as normal, changing the transition/rollback to work around the problems, stopping the transition and start rolling back, etc.

Using an example, the author once worked on a transition where some team members needed to travel into the office at weekend to perform some transition activity. Unfortunately, there was an issue with public transport which meant the individuals could not use it to travel. These cause a large amount of immediate panic and concern the transition would need to be abandoned. However, once the situation was reviewed it was easily resolved by arranging for a taxi to pick them up and drive them into the office and then home again once they had finished.

The poor management of problems when performing transitions and/or rollbacks could cause several problems. At one level, it could mean that the change is not transitioned into the live world smoothly. Also if the change is not transitioned fully or the rollback is not completed then it could cause wider implications for the day-to-day running of the business. The author once worked in an organisation that had problems with a major technology transition plan and they tried unsuccessfully to work their way through them. Regrettably, they did not start the rollback soon enough which mean the organisation's trading systems were not available until mid-day the following Monday. This caused massive issues for the organisation such as reputation issues, needing the fund client losses as well as some client legal disputes that are still in progress

There are some crumbs of comfort. Remember that if the transition plan and the rollback plans have been developed and tested thoroughly, then the Change Team and wider organisation should have confidence that both (a) the transition plan works and will successfully implement the change required and (b) the rollback plan can recover the change or organisation from any major or minor issues

Key Takeaways

- All change transition events will have problems despite the amount of testing and preparation performed

- Therefore the Change Team and other involved stakeholders (such as the Sponsor and Change Manager) need to beware are of this so they are mentally prepared.

- If problems are encountered then they need to manage with a 'cool head' to ensure no poor decisions are made which result in a change failure or wider organisational issues.

8.3 Follow the pre-agreed transition and rollbacks plan and only diverge from them with extreme caution.

It is important that the transition and rollback plans developed and tested earlier are followed exactly and any diverge from them is treated with extreme care and caution. The world is littered with change failures that have been caused by Change Teams not following the pre-agreed transition or rollback plans, or making changes to them without careful thought and consideration.

Transition and/or Rollback plan alternations should only be needed for a small range of serious or material reasons. One suitable reason is that there has been a problem or issue during the transition which can be addressed, at relatively low risk, by altering the plan. Plan alterations should not be made for ad-hoc reasons such as Change Team members deciding on the fly that they can do the tasks in better order or Change Team members deciding to skip tasks for some reasons.

This means that if the plans need to be changed then this must be thought about in great depth. The Change Team and other key stakeholders need to understand the issue that requires the plan to change, review any impacts that could happen and ensure all changes and associated risks are clearly understood and approved by the Sponsor, Steering Committee, subject-matter-experts and (if necessary) any involved clients and suppliers.

If there are major problems then it may be easier and safer to roll back the transition and start again later as opposed to trying to 'muddle' through them.

It is also important to remember that the transition and roll-back plans will have been tested thoroughly earlier and this should have given confidence that all the tasks, the dependencies are correct, control points work, the correct people are involved, etc. Therefore there should not be any reason to deviate from the plans significantly.

Key Takeaways

- Before any transition into a live environment is executed then a set of transition and rollback plans should have been developed and tested.

- These plans should provide comfort that the change can be transitioned to and rolled back if required

- Therefore Change Teams should only diverge from these plans in extreme circumstances (such as major unforeseen problems).

- But if it is necessary to change the plan then the plan alterations, their impact and associated risks need to be understood and signed off by the Sponsor, Steering Committee and (if necessary) the clients and suppliers.

8.4 Do not skip the control points within the transitions and roll-back plans.

As discussed earlier, all transition and rollback plans will include a set of control points. The purpose of these is to (a) track the progress of transition or rollback and also (b) provide an early indication of issues that could be developing such tasks are starting to run behind for a variety of reasons.

To recap; control Points can take two forms; namely:

- The first form is that a series of pre-agreed communications are issued. These are typically distributed by email, instant message or text message, to a pre-agreed list of stakeholders such as Change Team members, Steering Committee members and other individuals across the organisation, customers and/or suppliers. These updates will cover (a) progress against plan (b) problems encountered and how they are being managed and (c) any problems anticipated and how they are being mitigated.

- It is also advantageous to supplement these distributed updates with actual update meetings or calls. These should also cover a) progress against plan (b) problems encountered and how they are being managed and (c) any problems anticipated and how they are being mitigated. But, additionally, they give the advantage of (a) allowing any items to be discussed, debated and further clarification given and (b) these meetings can be used to make any decisions required such as signing off the change when it is completed or, if the change is hitting the point of no return, deciding to roll back.

However, these control points must not be skipped. There is often the tendency and temptation to skip these if the transition is progressing well, i.e. the transition is going well so why do we need to have these control points? Is not much better just to press ahead with the transition and stop wasting time on pointless updates and meetings? However, they must be followed; namely:

- These control points are in place to control and protect the transition, change and the Change Team. They are not pointless governance. A good parallel to this is the wearing of seat belts in cars. Just because one thinks they will not have an accident then this does not mean that one does not need to wear a safety belt. It is understood that is uncomfortable but it is there to protect you from yourself and other road users.

- It is important to remember that not all stakeholders will know the full details of the transition and they may need these updates and meetings to understand the progress being made and issues being encountered or anticipated. It will allow stakeholders to raise questions, challenge or request clarity on progress and any problems being encountered.

- They are good governance and it is a pre-agreed task plan. There it needs to be done.

- It ensures that senior stakeholders are aware of any current or possible future problems especially if these problems could jeopardize the transition or roll-back event. Apart from managing expectations, it will allow them to provide advice and steer on possible remediation actions and be ready to make any key decisions (such as changing the transition plan or authorising a roll-back).

Furthermore, it is important that when control points meetings are held or updates are communicated, all information is clear, factual and easy to read and follow. Issues or problems should not be 'spun' to make them sound better. This means the following:

- Key items should not be omitted from the updates especially if they are embarrassing.

- Problems should not be 'sugar coated' to make them sound less serious than they are.

- Remember senior management tend to get the top jobs through talent and they will be able to see through any spin or sugar-coating extremely quickly. If there is poor communication (especially if it is deliberate) then it will increase the amount of suspicion and reduce trust in eth Change Manager and Change Team.

Unfortunately, there is a long history of changes that ignored transition and rollback control points which meant issues were not trapped and/or managed and meant the change ultimately failed.

Key Takeaways

- All transition and roll-back plans will have a series of controls points to (a) ensure that the plan is progressing as intended and (b) to provide an indication of problems

- These are in place to control and change the transition, change and the Change Team so they must not be skipped or ignored.

- There is unfortunately a long history of changes that ignored transition and rollback control points which meant issues were not trapped and/or managed and meant the change ultimately failed.

8.5 Do not forget the point of no return.

As noted earlier (in section 7.9), all transition plans need a "Point of No Return" as one of their key control points on any transition activity. (While controls were covered as part of section 8.4 above, the "Point of No Return" is such an important control is worthwhile stressing it as a separate item).

To recap, the "Point of No Return" is the latest time that any rollback plan can be started to ensure that all rollback activity is completed in time to minimise any impact generally across the organisation. For example, using as a technology upgrade to an online ordering system. A system upgrade needs 12 hours to be rolled back. The online ordering systems must be available at 0600 on a Monday to ensure the organisations can perform their normal day-to-day business. If the system is not available then there would be material reputation, legal, customer and financial implications. This means the "Point of No Return" should be around 1600 on the previous Sunday because this would allow 12 hours to perform the rollback plus an extra 2 for contingency and comfort.

The key point to understand is that once the "Point of No Return" is passed and problems are, either, in progress or encountered, then there will not be sufficient time to fully complete the roll-back successfully to ensure the organisation can operate as normal and not impacted negatively in a wider context. For example, a late roll-back could result in key business functions and/or systems not being available for customers, suppliers, the general public, regulators, etc.

Therefore it is essential to track and monitor the "Point of No Return" very closely. For example:

- If problems are being encountered, and the transition is getting close to the "Point of No Return", then senior stakeholders (such as the Sponsor, Steering Committee plus others such as suppliers, regulators and clients) must be made aware of this (via the normal control point updates and meetings/calls mentioned in section 8.4)

    Depending on the circumstances, then these stakeholders may decide to start the rollback immediately because they are worried that problems in progress will not be fixed. This will ensure that the business is 'safe'.

    Alternatively, they may have confidence that the problems will be fixed and are happy to continue without rolling back. This has a risk element that the problems are not fixed which could mean either (a) a roll-back may need to be started at a later time or (b) the problems are fixed but the transition is completed later than planned. Both of these mean that the business may not be fully operating when its normal day-to-day business starts.

- Even if there are no problems and the "Point of No Return" is getting close then it is still important that the senior stakeholders (such as the Sponsor, Steering Committee and others such as suppliers, regulators and clients) are made aware of this via the normal control point updates and meetings/calls mentioned in section 8.4

They need to understand that if problems are encountered after this point has been reached then it cannot be guaranteed that any roll back activity will be completed in time.

Key Takeaways

- The "Point of No Return" is the latest date/time that a rollback can start to ensure that (a) the failed transition plan can be reversed and (b) the wider organisation is not impacted adversely by this failed transition.

- Therefore this point needs to be monitored proactively to ensure that stakeholders are aware when this date/time is near or passed so they can make any required decisions on whether to start a roll-back.

8.6 Is the Change Team being appreciated for their work and efforts?

(This question regarding appreciating people for their efforts is a common thread throughout the different stages of implementing change. This means that it appears a few times in this book. This has created some duplication but because this is an important point, then it is justified).

There is a tendency when performing a change transition into the live world to focus on the problems encountered and not thank people for their efforts and hard work and for completing activities.

Changes are stressful, require people to work long hours and can be demotivating if problems are being constantly discovered. This is particularly true when people are working long, tiring and stressful hours on a transition and/or roll-back.

Therefore it is important for the Sponsor, Change Manager, Steering Committee members and other senior managers to appreciate the efforts and achievements of the Change Team. For example, completing a phase of the change or agreeing on commercial terms with a new supplier. It makes the team feel appreciated and it also motivates them for the future. It is amazing the positive impact that a simple "thank you" or "well done" will have especially if it is unexpected and is received from a senior member of management. Therefore the Sponsor, Change Manager, Steering Committee members and other senior managers should be aware of the efforts of the Change Team and the achievements and send out "thank you" or "well done" messages to the relevant team members.

Key Takeaways

- Changes can be stressful especially if team members are working long hours and/or there is a constant wave of issues.

- The senior stakeholders need to appreciate the efforts and achievements of the Change Team.

- It makes the team feel appreciated and it also motivates them for the future.

- Therefore senior stakeholders should be aware of the efforts of the Change Team and the achievements and send out "thank you" or "well done" messages to the relevant team members as appropriate.

9 Remember that all changes need a certain amount of post-implementation support

> *"'Tis not enough to help the feeble up,*
> *but to support them after"*
> *- William Shakespeare*

9.1 Introduction

Even when a change is transitioned into live, then it will still require a certain amount of post-transition support. This means it is not a case of the change being transitioned into live and handed over to the business teams one day and then the Change Team being disbanded or walking away to join a new change the day after that.

Unfortunately, ensuring that changes are bedded in sufficiently, is a major part of ensuring change success. There are various examples where a change has not been bedded in properly and it has caused material problems with the running of the change. For example, issues were encountered that the business teams did not have the knowledge to address (because the Change Team have left) or there were software issues raised that were not fully understood (because, again, the Change Team were not available).

Therefore, it would be a shame to complete all the early parts of change perfectly but fail at this final stage.

The structure of this section is based on a list of questions. Each question focused on a particular problem that can hinder successful change and offers some guidance on how this area can be addressed.

9.2 Are all stakeholders aware that change takes time to bed in and this will mean the Change Team needs to be kept in place (often at a cost)

As mentioned earlier, it is a fact of change life that any transitioned or implemented change will take time to fully bed in. Changes that are not fully bedded are always problematic which could result in the change being unsuccessful as well as other problems.

This bedding in period is often referred to as the "warranty" or "hyper care" period and is required to cover some different items:

- There could be unforeseen problems that need to be fixed after go live.

  These could cover small issues such as process problems or simple software defects that can be resolved quickly. It is not uncommon for some changes to have emergency software bug fix releases already planned post-transition. If issues are uncovered then these pre-booked releases will be used to fix them. However, if the releases are not needed then they are cancelled.

  However, there could also be much larger issues such as major design issues or technical problems which will need the Change Team's knowledge, support and effort to resolve or workaround.

- The new business owner teams could be unclear or confused regarding any new procedures and processes. This is even true if everything has been fully tested, all staff have been trained and all changes are fully documented. Remember that things tend to be much scarier when things go live.

    Again having the Change Team available will provide a certain amount of support, comfort and guidance on managing problems.

    Therefore all senior stakeholders (such as the Sponsor, Steering Committee members, suppliers, customers, etc.) must be aware that the Change Team (or parts of it at least) will need to be kept in place post-transition to support any bedding in for a pre-agreed period. Apart from (a) tying up the Change Team and stopping them from working on new initiatives or even being let go, it will (b) incur a cost for the organisation and possibly any customers or suppliers involved. Although, these costs should have been covered by any earlier analysis and business case performed.

Key points

- All changes required a certain amount of bedding in post-transition.

- Therefore the Change Team (or parts of it) must be kept in place to provide any support required for a pre-agreed period

- All senior stakeholders will need to be aware of this because apart from (a) tying up the Change Team and stopping them from working on new initiatives or even being let go, it will (b) incur a cost for the organisation and possibly any impacted suppliers and customers.

9.3 Is there are a clear set of handover criteria to pass the ownership of change from the Change Team to the required business teams?

As mentioned previously, it is a fact of life that the Change Team will need to be in place to support the change immediately after to go live. Also as noted earlier, all senior stakeholders must be aware of this because it will impact change costs, staffing and resourcing.

However, having said that, the Change Team cannot support the change forever. This is because Change Teams can be very expensive, members of the Change Team may be required for other changes (or even let go if they are expensive consultants) and, ultimately, the business teams need to own the change at some point because ultimately it is their job.

This means that a clear set of handover criteria needs to be agreed, upon before transition, to determine when and how the change will formally pass from the Change Team to the business owners. If this criterion is not clear then it could result in confusion over ownership which could result in change failure.

The business owners can be viewed as two parts:

- First of all, there are the main or direct business owners who need to own any new processes, products, services etc. For example, if a new product is launched then it will need to be owned by the Product Management teams and/or the Sales teams.

- Secondly, there are indirect or supporting business owners. These groups tend to support the main or direct owners of the change as part of the normal day-to-day business running. For example, if a new product is launched that required technology changes to the ordering or stock control technology systems then it is important the technology teams who support these systems take ownership of any software changes from the Change Team.

There are no real 'hard and fast' rules for designing handover criteria because it depends on the organisation, the complexity of the change and the type of change. However, there are a couple of suggestions that can help. For example

- One suggestion is that all new processes, functions, etc. will need to have been successfully run at least once before ownership can be passed from the Change Team to the relevant business owners.

    For any new daily or weekly processes (such as trading or online ordering) then this should not be a problem because they can be all run within a few days of going live, and if there are any issues they can be raised and be addressed quickly.

    However, for any monthly, quarterly, half-yearly or annual processes, it will take a while to run them after go-live especially if any problems are encountered which need fixing. Therefore to avoid the costs and overheads of keeping the Change Team together then a pragmatic solution is often to disband the team once most of the daily processes have been completed but with the option of reforming them if there are any issues with these processes.

- A second suggestion is that some organisations will transfer staff members out of the Change Team into the business teams either on a temporary or permanent basis. This should ensure there is no loss of knowledge and migration is smooth, but it could increase the running costs for the business teams.

- A third option is time base where it could be agreed that the Change Team stays in place for a pre-agreed period. For example two weeks or one month following the transition date.

Key Takeaways

- While it is noted that the Change Team will need to support the transition change in the period just after go-live, the Change Team cannot support the change forever.

- This is because it is costly, the Change Team may be required for other changes (or even let go if they are expensive consultants) and, ultimately, the business teams need to own the change at some point.

- This means that a clear set of handover criteria needs to be agreed upon to determine when and how the change will pass from the Change Team to the business owners. If this criterion is not clear then it could result in confusion over ownership which could result in change failure.

9.4 Is the Change Team being appreciated for their work and efforts?

There is a tendency when supporting a previously transitioned change to focus on the problems encountered and not thank people for their efforts and hard work and for completing activities.

Changes are stressful, require people to work long hours and can be demotivating if problems are being constantly discovered. This is particularly true when people are working long, tiring and stressful hours on a transition and/or roll-back.

Therefore it is important for the Sponsor, Change Manager, Steering Committee members and other senior managers to appreciate the efforts and achievements of the Change Team. For example, completing a phase of the change or agreeing on commercial terms with a new supplier

It makes the team feel appreciated and it also motivates them for the future. It is amazing the positive impact that a simple "thank you" or "well done" will have especially if it is unexpected and is received from a senior member of management.

Therefore the Sponsor, Change Manager, Steering Committee members and other senior managers should be aware of the efforts of the Change Team and the achievements and send out "thank you" or "well done" messages to the relevant team members.

Finally, another noticeable way to provide a reward is to review the positive team member's performance and make this known to their managers. Changes are often not part of the employee's day job and there could be resentment on undertaking additional project tasks which are not going to impact the employees' reviews and appraisals.

Key Takeaways

- Changes can be stressful especially if team members are working long hours and/or there is a constant wave of issues.

- The senior stakeholders need to appreciate the efforts and achievements of the Change Team.

- It makes the team feel appreciated and it also motivates them for the future.

- Therefore senior stakeholders should be aware of the efforts of the Change Team and the achievements and send out "thank you" or "well done" messages to the relevant team members as appropriate.

10 There is still work to do even though the change is complete.

> *"An organization's ability to learn, and translate that learning into action rapidly, is the ultimate competitive advantage"*
> *- Jack Welch*

10.1 Introduction

Once a change is fully transitioned into production with all its post-transition support completed then it needs to be formally closed. This will allow the business owners to take full ownership of the change and for the Change Team to be completely disbanded.

If a change is not formally closed down then some changes have a habit of running on and on forever. This mean will that that the business owners will not take full ownership and often the (very expensive) Change Team is kept in place when they are not required, and organisations could continue to remain reliant on expensive external consultants.

It would be a shame to complete all the earlier parts of the change successful but fail on this final closure phase.

These closure activities cover several areas. Firstly it is important to assess whether the change was successful or not. It is also a good idea to perform some sort of lessons learnt review because, even for the most successful changes, there are good and bad lessons that can be learnt and taken into further changes. A formal closure report should be completed which lists any outstanding deliverables and who will own them now the Change Team is being disbanded. Finally, it is worthwhile to celebrate the success of the change. There is a tendency to focus on what went wrong or the problems encountered. However, celebrating success is good for staff motivation and morale as well as thanking people for their efforts and dedication.

The structure of this section is based on a list of questions. Each question focused on a particular problem that can hinder successful change and offers some guidance on how this area can be addressed.

10.2 Was the change been successful or not?

One could argue this is the most important part of implementing change – i.e. checking or confirming whether the changes implemented were successful or not?

At a high level, it is a simple case of reviewing the previously defined key success criteria and confirming whether they and the proposed business benefits have been met or not.

If everything looks fine and there are no issues then the Change Team can congratulate themselves.

However, if there are key success criteria that have not been met then it can be uncomfortable for the Change Team, Sponsor and Change Manager. If this happens then the reasons for this need to be understood. It will involve having an honest discussion within the Change Team, with suppliers, with customers and across the wider organisation to understand the following questions.

- Why were these not done?

- How important are these issues?

- What are the causes of these gaps?

- What is the impact of these key success criteria not being met?

This type of discussion needs a large amount of tact and good social skills by the Change Manager and Sponsor because it could easily evolve into finger-pointing and a blame passing exercise. It is important to have a cool and logical focus on the facts and their underlying causes. It is very easy to be distracted by rumours, opinions, half-truths or even outright lies.

Once there is a clear understanding of the gaps in the success criteria and what has caused them then the Change Team, Sponsor and wider organisation will need to understand what needs to be done to address them, namely:

- It may be necessary to keep the change running (albeit in a smaller state or using a further phase) until they are resolved. This will have implications on costs as well as tying up change and business staff for a future period.

- It may be decided that no further action is required and the organisation can cope with these success criteria not being met. If so then this would need approval from the Sponsor, Steering Committee and possibly other senior management, customers and suppliers.

- Alternatively, any gaps could be passed to different teams such as another change or into the business-as-usual teams to address as part of their normal day to day running. Again, this will need approval from the Sponsor, Steering Committee and possibly other senior management, customers and suppliers

Key Takeaways

- Once a change is completed then it needs to be assessed to understand whether it was successful or not.

- This can be done by reviewing the key success criteria to determine whether they have been met or not.

- If there are any gaps where the success criteria have not been met then it is important (a) to understand the reasons why (b) to understand the impact of these criteria not being met and then (c) to agree on how they should be managed going forward. Any decision made will need approval from the Sponsor, Steering Committee and possibly other senior management, customers and suppliers

10.3 Has a post-implementation review of the lessons learnt exercise been completed?

As mentioned several times earlier, one of the key reasons that organisations do not implement changes successfully (or even do not run their organisation well) is that they do not learn from their previous mistakes. They continue to make the same mistakes and errors over and over again.

Therefore, for any change, some type of post-implementation review exercise must be completed. This will allow the organisation to determine what went well and what could have been improved upon. These reviews should be completed regardless of whether the change was deemed successful or not.

It is also advisable to try and perform these reviews a couple of weeks after the change transitions into live or when all the post-transition support is completed. This is because it will ensure that the people involved in the change still feel the pain or the joy of the change which means they will be able to provide good feedback. If it is left any longer then people will quickly forget what happened and how they felt about the change.

Furthermore, these reviews must not become a blame game. This is very possible if the change had issues or problems and people may want to cover their positions, settle some scores, divert blame, or just play organisational politics. To avoid this then it is recommended that these reviews adhere to the following principles.

- A person (or coordinator) needs to be allocated to run the process. Normally it is the change Manager but sometimes, to avoid bias and conflicts of interest, the Sponsor may want to nominate a third party such as someone from Risk, Internal Audit or another Change Manager. For some large organisations and/or changes then somebody external (such as an auditor) could be employed.

- All feedback should be open and honest.

- All feedback should be as anonymous as possible because this will make people more willing to speak openly and honestly.

- All feedback should focus on facts and be supported by evidence. The review should try and steer away from rumours, opinions, gossip, half-truths and complete lies.

- Finally, the review should also look to cover what went well was just as what went badly. Remember, there are lessons to be learnt from items that went well. There is a tendency for these reviews to focus on what went badly.

To ensure there is some sort of control and structure, then the following five-step process can be followed by the coordinator.

- Initially, a questionnaire needs to be designed to gather feedback. This needs to cover the following three areas; (a) what went well and can be learned from this (b) what went badly and can be learned from this and (c) is there any other relevant comment and feedback

- This questionnaire will then need to be sent to all the people involved in the change. This can involve a wide range of people such as the Change Manager, the Change Team, the Sponsor, the Steering Committee, Business Teams, Customers, Suppliers and anyone else involved in the change.

- The people who received the questionnaire will need to complete and return it. This itself can be quite a chunky piece of work and there are some different ways to make this an easier process

  The easiest way is to obtain a written response which can be returned by email or some other electronic means. But because people are writing details down then they may feel a bit nervous about being open and honest. Any response could be guarded or heavily caveated.

  Another alternative is to hold either a single meeting or several meetings where the involved stakeholders can discuss feedback openly. However, some people may be nervous about speaking openly in a group especially if it could be seen to criticise somebody. Also, these meetings can easily be taken over by a dominant personality or a senior member of management if one attends.

  Probably the best option is 1-2-1 sessions with each of the involved stakeholders. These can either be via telephone, face-to-face or via video conference. This will allow people to be more open and honest. But on the downside, if there is a large number of people to speak to then it could take a long time to hold all the 1-2-1 sessions.

- Once all the questionnaires have been completed then it is a case of reviewing the responses and creating some sort of analysis and recommendations. Again, this work should focus on what went well, what went badly plus any other relevant feedback but with a particular focus on what lessons can be learnt going forward.

- Then once this is completed, the lessons learnt report can be presented to the Sponsor, Steering Committee and other stakeholders for review, challenge and approval. Depending on the feedback from these senior reviews then the recommendations may need to be enhanced.

- Once the recommendation has been signed off by senior management, then the lessons learnt report can be issued to all involved stakeholders for information

- Finally, the lessons learnt will need to be incorporated into the organisation's processes, procedures and behaviours to ensure they 'stick' and the issues are not repeated on future changes.

As the focus of these lessons learnt exercises is to try and ensure that the organisation does not repeat the same errors in the future then making these lessons 'stick' will require a large amount of proactive effort for all people across the organisation. This will range from the most junior members of staff to the most senior management and directors. There is a tendency for these reviews, once completed, to be filed away in a 'dusty drawer' and forgotten about. It is unclear why this happens to be honest but it could be due to people being content in their current ways of working and not seeing why changes are needed.

Key Takeaways

- One of the key reasons for change failure (and organisational problems generally) is not learning from their mistakes and then repeating the same mistakes continually.

- Therefore when a change is completed, some type of lessons learned or post-implementation review needs to be completed.

- When the output of this review is available then any lessons or recommendations fed back must be fed back into the organisation's processes, procedures and behaviours to ensure they 'stick' and the issues are not repeated on future changes.

10.4 Have all the successes been celebrated?

There is a tendency when implementing change or performing any post-change reviews, to focus on the problems encountered. This is key because an organisation needs to address any issues and fix them through lessons learned and self-learning

However, it is also important to celebrate success even if the change has not been 100% successful.

changes are stressful and require people to work long hours which means when a change is completed then it is important to recognise the effort put in by team members for a variety of reasons. It makes them feel appreciated and it also motivates them for the future. It is amazing the positive impact that a simple "thank you" will have.

But celebrating success does need a little amount of thought to ensure it matches the culture of the Change Team, the individuals within it and the organisation widely. For example:

- One of the best methods is an individual email sent from the Sponsor (or somebody else senior) sent to each team member to thank them individually for their efforts. For example "thank you for long hours ensuring all the legal work was completed" or "thank you for your dedication in ensuring all the new software changes are tested thoroughly". This could result in a large amount of work in issuing these emails but the individual personal nature of each email will be appreciated by the Change Team members.

- A second option is for the Sponsor (or somebody else senior) to issue some type of Change Team wide or even organisational wide email, thanking everyone for the work on the change. Again this is useful but it does lack the personal touch of individual emails. Also if it is worded poorly then can seem to be very cheesy and patronising.

- Some organisations also look to give some type of gift. This can range anything from a box of biscuits to a pen, to a book voucher. Some organisations also donate extra paid day's holiday as a thank you gift. But it is important to think carefully about the type of gift because the Change Team wants to find a gift that everybody likes and does not feel patronising. Also if the organisation gives out gifts for one change when it completes then it needs to do the same for all changes when they complete.

- One other common type of celebration is to hold a social event or party. This is often a popular option but it is key to remember that some people do not like social events and they might feel uncomfortable at a party. Furthermore, if the Change Team is spread across multiple locations or time zones then either it may not be possible for everyone to attend, or multiple social events may need to be held.

- Finally, another method to provide a reward is to review the positive team member's performance and make this known to their manager. Changes are often not part of the employee's day job and there could be resentment on undertaking additional project tasks which are not going to impact the employees' reviews and appraisals.

Key Takeaways

- There is a tendency to focus on issues and problems when a change has been implemented

- However, it is important to celebrate any success to ensure that people's efforts are recognised, that they appreciated and to ensure they are motivated them going forward.

- Therefore when a change completes then the Sponsor, Change Manager and other senior management need to thank the team for their efforts.

- There are various options regarding how this can be done ranging from a simple 'thank you' email to a large social event. However, any recognition needs to ensure it fits in with the culture of the Change Team and the organisation.

10.5 Has the change been formally closed?

Now all the change activities have been completed, a formal change closure report needs to be completed. Once closed, the Change Team can be disbanded (and moved to other changes or let go if they are external contractors or consultants) and the ownership of the change will move the new nominated business owners.

Unless there is a formal process to close a change then there is a tendency for changes to keep running forever and ever. While this may not cause a problem regarding the change is a success or not, it will be a drain and drag on organisational resources.

The closure document will typically contain the main parts.

1. A summary of how successful the change was with any gaps and issues noted. (In effect a summary of section 10.2).

2. A summary of the lessons learnt with any recommendations. (In effect a summary of section 10.3).

3. A list of what needs activities are outstanding. When a change completes, there is always a list of issues outstanding such as process problems that need addressing, software fixes that will need correcting, problems with migrated data etc. These items need to be listed with whom or who will own when the change formally closes.

This report needs to be formally reviewed and signed off by the Sponsor and Steering Committee. The formal sign-off of this document will formally trigger the change closing.

As part of this closure phase, there will also be a certain amount of change housekeeping. This is to ensure that all documents, emails, reports, analysis, etc. are stored in a central document repository or folder so they are not lost and are easy to find if required. For example, they could be required for general reference, input into future changes, needed for audit/risk reviews etc. The Change Manager should ensure that this is completed before they 'step down'.

Key Takeaways

- When a change completes then a formal change closure report should be completed which will trigger the end of the change.

- This document will need to contain lessons learnt, gaps in the success criteria and a list of who owns the completion of any outstanding task.

- This document would also need to be formally approved and signed off by the Steering Committee and Sponsor.

- Also as part of this closure phase, there needs to be some housekeeping where all documents, emails, reports, etc. need to be stored in a central repository to allow easy access if required in the future.

11 Conclusion and closing points

"Focus on the journey, not the destination. Joy is found not in finishing an activity but in doing it".
- Greg Anderson

Change is challenging, stressful and hard work to implement successfully. Many changes initiatives have had all manner of problems and issues. For example, cost overruns, delays in delivery dates, missing functionality, functionality that does not work, etc. (Remember that this level of failure is despite an entire industry in situ to try and improve the record of change success. This industry itself covers many areas such as consultants, books, training, professional qualifications, etc.).

Nevertheless, it is very possible to deliver change successfully and many organisations do deliver very complex and challenging change which delivers real and excellent benefits to the organisation itself as well as their customers, their suppliers, the wider environment etc.

This book has covered many areas to organisations improve their record of change in a very sequential process. It starts from ensuring the organisation has the correct capabilities to implement change, it then discusses preparing for the change, it then covers executing the change, followed by transitioning the change into the live world and ensuring the change is safely closed down.

However, there are some key themes that 'cut across' the sequential stages or steps listed above and these are listed below for completeness

- Ensure the change links to a key business reason. Be wary of making a change without a clear business reason or benefit.

- Ensure your organisation has the capabilities, skills, etc., to implement successful change. Organisations without these capabilities will struggle to implement change successfully.

- Change by nature is messy and chaotic. Therefore it needs structure around it to control and manage it

- Change requires a large number of 'things' to be implemented to allow it to be implemented. Therefore the devil is in the detail which means it is important to be paranoid about implementing change and constantly (a) check for issues, problems, omissions, delays, etc., as well as (b) plan or forecast forward to ensure an organisation, is always on the front-foot.

- Change is a human process and therefore do not forget or neglect the human element otherwise it will cause issues.

- Change is hard-work, stressful and challenging which means people need to work long hours to complete the change. Therefore remember to appreciate the efforts of the change team. A simple "thank you" goes a long way.

Therefore, to close the book, it is hoped that some of the ideas, questions, hints-and-tips and guidance listed in this book will help organisations improve their record of change and therefore provide benefits to thee organisations, their customer, their suppliers and wider society.

Paul Taylor
March 2022

A – Checklist summary

It is recognised that there is a large amount of detail within this book that could be challenging to follow and use pragmatically. Therefore this checklist or summary has been created to provide an overview of all the points raised earlier in this book

A.1 - Does the organisation have the capability to make changes successfully?

INTERNAL ISSUES

a) Ref #4.2 - Has the organisation grown by acquisition?

- Growth by acquisition is a part of organisational life and it is unlikely something that Change Team can address on their own,
- However, it is important to identify any issues here because any associated complexity will need to be catered for in the change plan, budget and other change elements.
- It is also worthwhile ensuring the Steering Committee and Sponsor are aware of these problems so they can help if required

b) Ref #4.3 - How much autonomy from the parent does the organisation have?

- The lack of empowerment is another fact of business life that the Change Team will struggle to fix themselves.

- However, if it does happen then it will cause issues with implementing change successfully.
- If this is noted then the Change Manager needs to raise this with the Sponsor and Steering Committee to ensure that they are aware of any problems that this could cause.
- However, some options can be used to provide some sort of mitigation such as requesting more autonomy, asking for pre-approvals, involving staff from the parent organisation and delegated decision making.

c) Ref #4.4 - How silo'ed is the organisation?

- Working with organisations with silos again is another factor of organisational life and it is something that the Change Team is very unlikely to address themselves.
- The best mitigation is to involve representation from each 'silo' within the Change Team. But for a large change spread across a large number of silos, this could be challenging.
- Regardless of any complexities around this will need to be included in the change plan, budget, issues, staffing etc.
- Finally, the Steering Committee and Sponsor must be also aware of any challenges in this area and whether these are causing any problems to the change being implemented.

d) Ref #4.5 - How well is the Missions Statement and Strategic Direction understood?

- All Organisations and firms should have a mission statement.
- The purpose of a mission statement is to provide some sort of steer and understanding concerning why the organisation exists.
- All stakeholders (covering internal, suppliers, customers and others) should understand the mission statement of an organisation. If there are gaps in the knowledge then these need

to be addressed immediately.
- All stakeholders involved in a change should understand how the change fits in with the Mission Statement.
- This clear understanding helps with implementing change successfully, and it will ensure that changes that do not match the missions statement are either stopped or enhanced to ensure it does match

e) Ref #4.6 - How well does the organisation react to Market and Industry changes?

- Organisations that react quicker and better to change in the market and industry will implement change more successfully
- However, if issues are noted in this area then there is very little the individual Change Team could do about this.
- Any problems should be escalated (both tactfully and on a one-to-one basis) to the Sponsor, senior management and Steering Committee members so they can take some holistic organisational-wide action

f) Ref #4.7 - How much customer focus does the organisation have?

- Organisations that have a real customer focus (for both external and internal customers) will implement change more successfully
- However, if issues are noted in this area then there is very little the individual Change Team could do about this.
- Any problems should be escalated (both tactfully and on a one-to-one basis) to the Sponsor, senior management and Steering Committee members so they can take some holistic organisational-wide action

g) Ref #4.8 - How well does the organisation learn from their mistakes?

- All organisations say they learnt from their mistakes but there is clear evidence that organisations do not always do this.
- Organisations that do learn from their mistakes both (a) run their organisations much better and (b) implement change successfully.
- If the Change Manager and Change Team are worried about mistakes being repeated then two routes can be followed.
- Firstly they can gather data on previous 'errors' which help define the change going forward. This data can be obtained via previous change post mortems and tactfully speaking to people.
- Secondly, it would be advantageous to escalate (both tactfully and on a one-to-one basis) any larger problems discovered to the Sponsor, senior management and Steering Committee members

h) Ref #4.9 - How much empowerment do staff have to make decisions?

- Organisations that give staff empowerment to make decisions and to do their job without unreasonable controls tend to be run much more effectively (including implementing change more successful).
- If there is insufficient empowerment then may be possible (with the agreement of the Sponsor and other senior management) to temporarily allow more empowerment within the change.
- Regardless the Sponsor will need to be fully aware of any issues regarding this and what problems they cause with the change.

i) Ref #4.10 - How supportive and knowledgeable are senior management?

- Without suitably skilled senior management support then a change will almost indefinitely fail.
- One could argue there is no point starting at change unless senior management are suitably skilled
- However, if there are gaps then there is very little the Change Team can do at the organisation-wide level apart from tactfully ensuring the Sponsor and Steering Committee are aware.
- But there are some mitigating options at the individual change level which can be actions For example spending more time with senior management, explaining issues in more detail or looking to temporarily recruit experts.

j) Ref #4.11 - How well does the organisation's culture manage the human aspects?

- Any human factor related issues must be identified and addressed urgently otherwise they will grow into major issues which result in the change failing.
- Unfortunately, it is very challenging to manage human issues and most people, including Change Managers, will feel very uncomfortable about tackling them but it is, unfortunately, part of the job.
- At the organisation level, it is very hard for an individual Change Manager to fix anything if there are major human factor issues. These issues are part of the wider organisation and senior management will need to address these. However it would be worthwhile for the Change Manager to tactfully express concerns to the Sponsor so they can work with senior management to address them.
- However, some improvements could be made by the Change Manager to help smooth the change running.

k) Ref #4.12 - Does the organisations have an organisation-wide committee to oversee all changes that are either planned or in progress?

- All organisations must have some type of change management processes and procedures in place.
- As part of this, every organisation must have a "Senior Organisation-wide Change Oversight Committee" that will oversee all changes progress across the organisation.
- This committee will track progress and issues as well as ensure the organisation deploys its limited change capacity on the most important changes and in the most effective way.
- Organisations without a Senior Organisation-wide Change Oversight Committee will struggle to implement change successfully. This is because they will not formally track progress at a senior level, issues will be missed and the organisation will not use its resources most effectively.

l) Ref #4.13 - Does the organisations have an organisation-wide Change Management process that can be used for all Changes that need to be made?

- All organisations must have some type of change management processes and procedures in place.
- Another part of this is that a clear and understood Change management process is in place that each Change in progress can follow.
- Without this, the Change Managers may not have the tools to run changes and also there will not be consistency across changes are made. The result is confusion with an increased probability of change failure

m) Ref #4.14 - Does the organisations have an organisation-wide Change Control process to manage changes in scope, timelines, etc. for inflight changes?

- All organisations must have some type of change management processes and procedures in place.
- This means there should also be an organisational-wide Change Control Process to review any changes to scope, timeline and costs on an in-flight change.
- The purpose of this is to ensure all alterations are assessed, reviewed and approved (or rejected) by the required management forums.
- Without this in place then alterations will be made 'on the fly' which will (a) result in individual changes either having issues or even failing and (b) result in the organisation not managing all the individual changes in progress effectively.

n) Ref #4.15 - Are the various Change Management processes a good 'cultural' fit for the organisation?

- As noted several times earlier all organisations must have some type of change management processes and procedures in place.
- However, these must match the culture and the context of the organisation
- A poor cultural or context fit could result in change problems and possibly even failure.

o) Ref #4.16 - What should an organisation do if they do not have any or insufficient Change Management processes?

- As mentioned several times earlier (especially in sections 4.12 to 4.15), all organisations must have some type of change management processes and procedures in place.

- If it is not in place, then one needs to be implemented whether at an organisation level or something specific is created just for the change in question.

p) Ref #4.17 - How susceptible is the organisation to the latest management and/or change 'fads'?

- The latest management new ways of working can provide real benefits to organisations and their stakeholders.
- However, it is important to ensure that organisations understand the benefits before they are implemented.
- Otherwise, it will cause problems with the organisations and impact its ability to implement change successfully

EXTERNAL ISSUES

q) Ref #4.18 - How regulated is the environment that the organisation operates in?

- To be honest, not much can be done about the amount of regulation in the industry. It is a fact of life working within those industries.
- However, when making changes, it is important to ensure that the change understands the regulatory impact because it could impact the likelihood of success. These impacts will need to be reflected in change plans, costs, activity, etc.
- All stakeholders (such as Sponsors and Steering Committee members) must be aware of the regulatory 'drag' with the change and the associated possible impacts.

r) Ref #4.19 - How complex is the client base?

- All organisations have a complex set of clients. It is a fact of organisational life.
- It is important to understand the complexity of the client base otherwise it will make implementing successful change more challenging.
- If this complexity is not fully understood then further analysis is required although hopefully, it should be a reasonably simple piece of work.
- Any complexity (or gaps in knowledge) need to be factored in the change and the Steering Committee and other senior management need to be aware.
- Finally, depending on the client's impact by the change, then it may be worthwhile to involve clients (either directly or via internal client-facing teams) in the change.

s) Ref #4.20 - How complex is the set of products and/or services offered?

- All organisations have a complex set of products and services. It is a fact of organisational life. The bigger the organisation then the wider and more complex range of products and services that will be offered.
- It is important to understand the complexity of the product and service base otherwise it will make implementing successful change more challenging.
- If this complexity is not fully understood then further analysis is required although hopefully, it should be a reasonably simple piece of work.
- Any complexity (or gaps in knowledge) need to be factored in the change and the Steering Committee and other senior management need to be aware.
- Finally, depending on the client's impact by the change, then it may be worthwhile to involve individuals from the product and service ownership teams directly in the change.

HYBRID INTERNAL AND EXTERNAL ISSUES

t) Ref #4.21 - How well is the operating model understood?

- Complex operating models are a fact of life, especially for certain businesses. It is not something that any Change Team is likely to fix in their timescales.
- However, the Change Team must understand the complexity of the operating model, especially those elements that are impacted by the change. For example, which components and integrations will be impacted by the change?
- If there are gaps in this knowledge then they must be addressed before the change starts, otherwise, it will cause problems.
- Also, senior management should be made aware of these issues with any associated implications.

u) Ref #4.22 - It is important to ensure that consistent terminology is used across all stakeholders.

- Change management and individual industries (such as Education or Technology) have a wide range of differing, complex and confusing terms and definitions.
- Therefore, to avoid any confusion and unnecessary problems, then it is important to agree on a consistent set of terms and definitions for all stakeholders (such as internal parties, external suppliers, customers, regulators, etc.) covering both Change Management and the industry where the change is being implemented

A.2 - Has sufficient pre-planning work been performed?

INITIAL THINKING

a) Ref #5.2 - Is it clear what has triggered the change?

- If it is unclear what has triggered a change, then an organisation should immediately stop the change and review the situation immediately with the relevant senior management.
- An organisation should not proceed with a change unless it is crystal clear what has triggered the change and how the change supports the organisation's strategy.
- It is also important to constantly review the change triggers during implementation to ensure they are still valid. If not then the change may become void and may not be required.
- Otherwise, the change will almost definitely fail.

b) Ref #5.3 - Is it clear what the business case for the change is?

- If it is unclear what the business case or benefits of a change are to organisations then they should stop the change immediately and review the situation with the relevant senior management.
- An organisation should not proceed with a change unless it is clear what the business benefits are how they match the organisation's strategy.
- Otherwise, the change will fail.

c) Ref #5.4 - Is it clear who will benefit from the change?

- It is understood who benefits from a change then it will allow the organisation to link it closer to the Mission Statement and be motivated to complete it.
- If it is not possible to clearly define who benefits then there could be issues with the business case
- If so then further will be needed to confirm who will benefit.
- No change should proceed unless it is clear who benefits from the change.

d) Ref #5.5 - Is there a clearly defined and agreed set of success criteria?

- It is essential that each change has a clearly defined and agreed set of success criteria because otherwise how is it possible to determine whether a change is successful or not?
- Therefore if a change is running or about to start and there is no clearly defined and agreed set of success criteria then change needs to stop immediately until this resolved
- No change should progress unless it is possible to measure whether it is successful or not.

e) Ref #5.6 - Is there a clear vision of the end-state (or what the world will look like once the change is implemented)?

- Completing a documented vision of the end-state is a good idea because it will ensure there is a focus, provides a safety net, helps with implementation and is a good communication aid.
- However, if it is not possible to document this vision then this perhaps the change is not fully understood.
- This means further investigation is required to understand the change, what is triggering it, why it is required, what are the success criteria etc.

f) Ref #5.7 - Is there an understanding of what the Business Requirements for the Change are?

- The requirements for change should be documented as much as possible at the start of the change
- The process of gathering requirements is a specific discipline and therefore should only be performed by suitably skilled individuals.
- However, there will be gaps that will need to be filled by assumptions or estimates with tasks in place to address them as quickly as possible. The relevant change documentation needs to be updated to reflect this.
- Furthermore, all stakeholders, especially the Sponsor and Steering Committee, need to be fully away of any gaps in the requirements.
- However, if it is still not possible to document even a basic list of requirements of what is needed then it is likely that the change is not fully understood.
- This needs to be addressed urgently because a change should proceed without an understanding of the requirements

g) Ref #5.8 - Has a suitable amount of money been allocated to the change?

- At the start of the change, it should be possible to create an initial budgetary amount, albeit with some known gaps, caveats and a level of probability
- If it is not possible to do this then it could be a symptom of wider issues. For example, the scope, plan, etc. are not fully understood. If so then is recommended that the Change Team investigates the scope, list of changes, timeline, etc. to ensure they understand it in more depth.
- No changes should proceed without at least having an indicative budget

h) Ref #5.9 - Does the organisation understand the complexity of the change being implemented?

- Reviewing the complexity of a change before it started a massive safety check.
- If an organisation underestimates the complexity of a change then it could fail.
- Organisations need to look themselves in the mirror and ask themselves "Now we have understood the scope, timelines, plans, etc., do we understand the complexity of change?"
- This is especially true if the organisation has not done a similar change before
- It is better to challenge oneself now before the change starts, and make adjustments, as opposed to starting the change and encountering major issues when the change is running.
- Even if the Change Team do feel they fully understand the complexity of the change then it is still advisable to proceed with caution and constantly review the situation.

i) Ref #5.10 - All changes will have a large number of problems and the stakeholders must be aware of this?

- Change is a complex subject and despite having the best plans in place there will be problems.
- Therefore, to manage expectations, all senior management must be aware of this.

PLANNING

j) Ref #5.11 - Is there an understanding of what 'things' need to be changed to implement the change?

- The scope of a change should be documented at the start of the change as much as possible

- However, there will be gaps that will need to be filled by assumptions or estimates with change tasks in place to address them as quickly as possible. The relevant change documentation needs to be updated to reflect this.
- Furthermore, all stakeholders, especially the Sponsor and Steering Committee, need to be fully away of any gaps in scope.
- However, if it is still not possible to document even a basic scope of what needs to be changed then it is likely that the change is not fully understood.
- This needs to be addressed urgently because a change should proceed without an understanding of the scope and issues.

k) Ref #5.12 - Is there an understanding of how the change will be transitioned into the live environment?

- Having an idea of the transition approach as early as possible will help with planning the change and it will set expectations with stakeholders (such as the Sponsor, Steering Committee, suppliers, customers and even regulators). They should object at the start of the change when everything is still very much in the planning stage, then when work on the transitions is actually in progress.
- If an organisation or a change, is struggling even to think about how the change could be transitioned at even a high level then it could be a sign that they do not understand the change in sufficient detail.
- This is a sign of trouble and the change should investigate the change in more detail before proceeding.

l) Ref #5.13 - Has an initial change plan (even if draft) been completed?

- Creating a plan at the start of a change should always be attempted but there will always be issues (especially for the larger and more complex changes).

- It should be possible to define the main tasks or chunks of work, their dependencies, the resources required to implement them, any key dates and the critical path.
- It should also be possible to highlight any gaps, issues or unknowns as part of this change.
- However, if it is not possible to create even a simple then this could be the symptom of something more significant.
- If so then further work should be completed to understand the triggers of the change, the reason for the change, the business justification, etc.
- A change should not proceed without some sort of plan (even if it is a draft with some issues outstanding)

GOVERNANCE

m) Ref #5.14 - Does the change have an appropriate Sponsor?

- It cannot be stressed enough that the selection of a suitable Sponsor is essential.
- If the change is successful then the Sponsor can take the plaudits but if the change is unsuccessful then the Sponsor will need to take full responsibility. This failure could result in disciplinary action or even sometimes dismissal from the organisation.
- The world is scattered with failed changes that did not have the correct Sponsor.
- If there is any concern about the selection of the Sponsor then this needs to be addressed with senior management immediately before the change progresses too far.

n) Ref #5.15 - Is there suitable senior management oversight and forums in place?

• There must be some type of senior forum to oversee, challenge and steer the change. Otherwise, there is a real chance that the change will miss issues and/or not receive the support required which will result in a change failure.
• The forum (a) must contain the required members (b) meets as frequently as required and (c) receive the correct inputs.
• If an organisation is struggling to determine who needs to sit on this forum then it is probably a sign that the change is not fully understood. Therefore further work is required with the Sponsor on understanding impacts, what needs to change, timelines and who needs to be involved
• No change should proceed without a senior oversight forum.

o) Ref #5.16 - Is there a suitable Change Manager in place?

• The selection of a suitable Change Manager is essential (although this role can sometimes call Project Manager, Programme Management or Portfolio Manager).
• If the wrong person is selected then the change will fail.
• Therefore it is best to spend as much time on the selection as possible.
• However, if there is a change up and running at the moment in the Change Manager is a bad fit then there are two options for the Sponsor or other senior manager. Either (a) the Change Manager is removed and replaced or (b) they should be given more support from either other change and/or the Sponsor.

p) Ref #5.17 - Is there an appropriate communication strategy in place?

• Good, frequent, accurate and open communication is essential because all stakeholders are aware of what is happening.

- If communication is poor or stakeholders are not aware of what is happening, then this could cause problems, result in damaging rumours being formed, create an amount of scepticism and reduce the likelihood that the change will succeed

q) Ref #5.18 - Have suitable processes and controls been implemented?

- To maximise the chance of a change being successful then there needs to be some type of suitable processes with controls.
- This will ensure that all key tasks are done, progress is tracked, issues are managed etc.
- A good process can be seen as a good safety net to trap issues.
- If there is no process in place then there is a good chance that the change will be chaotic and therefore not succeed fully. In this case, then the Change Manager, Sponsor and Change Team to put one in place.

r) Ref #5.19 - Have all issues, ambiguities and gaps have been logged at the start of the change?

- This is another safety check before a change starts 'proper'.
- All changes will have a long list of issues, gaps and unknowns at the start.
- Therefore it is good to constantly challenge oneself to ensure all issues, gaps, etc. are noted for future resolution.
- Remember, it is much better to waste a couple of hours of effort at the start of the change to ensure the issue is correct than to proceed and encounter problems that could take a while to address when the change is running.
- As noted above, the mismanagement of issues is a key contributor to failed changes.

WHO NEEDS TO BE INVOLVED AS PART OF THE CHANGE TEAM?

s) Ref #5.20 - Is it clear what people, teams and organisations need to be involved in implementing the change.

- Documenting a detailed list of who needs to be involved in the change is essential.
- This list of people could in-house people, suppliers, customers, regulators plus many others.
- Some organisations use a tool called a RACI matrix to record this.
- Changes that do not have this list with almost definitely fail.
- If the Change Manager and Sponsor has a good understanding of the scope, plan and triggers then it should be possible to create a list.
- However, if it is not possible to identify who needs to be involved then the change has a problem and further work is required to understand the change triggers, plan and scope.
- It would be unwise to proceed very far in the change without knowing who needs to be involved.

t) Ref #5.21 - Is there a suitable works stream structure in place to ensure the change is delivered?

- At this stage of the change, it should be possible to create a workstream structure covering the 'chunks' of work or tasks required.
- This structure is required to ensure there is some sort of control to manage the complex and chaotic nature of change.
- If this structure is not in place or the structure is not fit for purpose, then the change will fail.
- Therefore, if it is not possible to define the structure in any detail, then the Change Team may have some issues. It would be advisable to perform some further analysis regarding the scope, plan and the people/teams that need to be involved.

u) Ref #5.22 - Have the required internal staff been included in the Change Team?

- To ensure that any change is implemented correctly then it needs to correct people involved at the right time. If people are not involved or involved too late then the change will fail
- However, if a change is still struggling to understand what people need to be involved then this is a symptom of earlier issues? Therefore further work is required regarding the scope, plan and which people need to be involved.
- It is dangerous to proceed with a clear understanding of who needs to be involved.

v) Ref #5.23 - Does the organisation have the required skill sets in place?

- Once it is understood what internal teams are needed, then it is a good idea to do a final 'safety net' check to ensure they have the required skills.
- If they do not then they need to be filled before the implementation of the change starts.
- This can be done in several ways. For example, training, seconding internal experts if available, or bringing in external specialists

w) Ref #5.24 - Have all the required external suppliers being engaged in the change.

- To ensure that any change is implemented successfully it needs the relevant external suppliers involved when they are required. If the correct suppliers are not involved or involved too late then the change will fail
- The process of engaging a supplier can take some time to complete a vendor selection process and any legal negotiations.

Therefore sufficient time needs to be included in plans.
- However, if a change is still struggling to determine what external suppliers need to be involved then this could be a symptom of issues. Therefore further work is required around the scope, plan and which external suppliers need to be involved.
- It is dangerous to proceed with a clear understanding of what external suppliers need to be involved

x) Ref #5.25 - Have the required Internal or intragroup suppliers being engaged in the change.

- To ensure that any change is implemented successfully it needs the relevant intragroup suppliers involved as and when they are required.
- If the correct intragroup suppliers are not involved or involved too late then the change will fail
- Engaging intragroup suppliers can take a while due to internal engagements and prioritisation processes. Therefore the Sponsor may be required to help if this is starting to impact deadlines.
- However, if a change is struggling to determine what intragroup suppliers need to be involved then this could be a symptom of issues. Therefore further work is required about the scope, plan and which intragroup suppliers need to be involved.
- It is dangerous to proceed with a clear understanding of what intragroup suppliers need to be involved.

y) Ref #5.26 - Have all required customers been engaged in the change?

- To ensure that any change is implemented successfully then it may need to involve its customers.
- This involvement can either directly include the customers or include them indirect by (say) an internal customer-facing team.

It is also a good idea to have an emergency communication plan in place to mitigate the issue if customers hear about the change before they are formally communicated.
- However, if a change is still struggling to determine whether and what customers need to be involved then this is an indicator of issues. Therefore further work is required concerning the scope, plan and what customers need to be involved in.
- It is dangerous to proceed with a clear understanding of what customers need to be involved in. It would be very embarrassing if an organisation did not realise that they had to include customers until towards the end of the change and then they had quickly involved the customers at the last minute.

z) Ref #5.27 - Has the required infrastructure for the change been put in place?

- All changes will require some sort of physical and virtual infrastructure in place so the change can be delivered. This infrastructure will cost money so it All changes need some type of infrastructure to operate. The costs of this will need to be factored into the change costs.
- If there are any material gaps in the required infrastructure then this could cause problems. If so then this needs to be discussed with the Sponsor and possibly the Steering Committee.
- Changes that have large gaps in the required infrastructure will fail.

SAY THANK YOU

aa) Ref #5.28 - Is the Change Team being appreciated for their work and efforts?

- Changes can be stressful especially if team members are

working long hours and/or there is a constant wave of issues.
- The senior stakeholders need to appreciate the efforts and achievements of the Change Team.
- It makes the team feel appreciated and it also motivates them for the future.
- Therefore senior stakeholders should be aware of the efforts of the Change Team and the achievements and send out "thank you" or "well done" messages to the relevant team members as appropriate.

A.3 - Is the change being implemented in the most appropriate manner?

a) Ref #6.2 - How supportive and knowledgeable are senior management?

- Changes without support from senior management will fail. This is unfortunately a common reason for failure.
- If there are areas of concern in this area, then the Change Manager will need to speak to the Sponsor, Steering Committee as well as their fellow senior managers to try and address this issue. This will not be an easy conversation.
- There are various options to address these problems (such as involving different management or temporarily recruiting experts).
- But if these problems persist then, at best, the change should proceed with caution especially if there are tight deadlines, or, at worse, the change should either pause or slow down until the issue is addressed.

b) Ref #6.3 - How well are the Change Manager and the Sponsor working together?

- The Change Manager and a Sponsor is a key working relationship and it must work

- There are many examples of changes failing because of a poor relationship between the two.
- If there are problems then they need to be addressed immediately.

c) Ref #6.4 - Are the correct number of issues being raised for the size of the change?

- This is another key safety net check
- If the Change Team is working on a large change then they should have a large number of complex issues.
- If the Change Team does not have this then it could be a sign of problems such as not fully understanding the change or items are being missed.
- Therefore it is recommended that the Change Team perform a deep dive into the changes to confirm all issues have been identified

d) Ref #6.5 - Does the change 'feel' like is progressing well?

- A good indicator of change problems is to ask all stakeholders how they 'feel' the change is progressing.
- If this 'gut feel' feedback matches the tracking of the change then this is fine but if there is a difference then this needs to be investigated.
- The differences may not be significant but it could be an indicator of problems that, if not addressed, could result in the change failing.

e) Ref #6.6 - How well are change issues and problems being managed?

- The old saying "a stitch in time saves nine" is so very true here.

- If issues are managed proactively and effectively then it will reduce the likelihood of change failure.
- If issues appear to be left unmanaged or left to drift then the Change Manager will need to take immediate urgent action to address this.

f) Ref #6.7 - Are Change Team members working constantly long hours?

- While team members constantly working long hours could be due to the stage the change is at, it is worthwhile checking in just in case because it could be a symptom of a problem with a change.
- Also working long hours negatively impact staff work-life balances which in turn will cause personal issues.
- Therefore if there are issues they need to be addressed as soon as possible.

g) Ref #6.8 - Is the governance structure in place still fit-for-purpose now the change is up and running?

- If the governance for the change is not fit-for-purpose then it will not control the change as required and it could contribute to change failure.
- If problems are discovered then the Change Manager will need to work with the Change Team, Sponsor, Steering Committee and other key stakeholders to address them urgently.

h) Ref #6.9 - Are key decisions being made as and when they are needed?

- Decision making (especially at the strategic or senior level) is key and must be made timely.

- The world is plagued with many failed changes which were caused by delayed or slow decision making.
- Some decisions can be made within the Change Team and should be easier to manage.
- However, more key decisions will need to be made by senior stakeholders. These must be made promptly. This means it is essential that the decision-makers are (a) aware they need to make a decision (b) know by when they need to make and (c) are provided with sufficient data/information to allow them to make the decision.

i) Ref #6.10 - How well is resistance being identified and managed during the change?

- All change will have resistance but is important that any resistance is understood and managed.
- If it is ignored then it will fester and then cause further problems which could be disastrous for the change.
- Therefore it is important that Change Teams actively search out resistance, understand its cause, assess its impacts and then manage it accordingly.

j) Ref #6.11 - How much re-planning is taking place during implementation?

- Re-planning is a necessary part of implementing change.
- But if there is a constant flow of plan changes then this could be an indication of something more serious.
- If so then it would be worthwhile for the Change Manager in conjunction with the Sponsor and Change Team to completely review the change it is entirely

k) Ref #6.12 - How effective is the stakeholder communication strategy?

- Good, frequent, accurate and open communication is essential because all stakeholders are aware of what is happening.
- This covers both (a) outbound communication to provide updates etc. plus (b) allow stakeholders to raise inbound communication into the Change Team to allow them to raise issues and questions.
- Remember that it may be necessary to perform different communications approaches for different stakeholder groups.
- If communication is poor or stakeholders are not aware of what is happening, then this could cause problems, result in damaging rumours being formed, create an amount of scepticism and reduce the likelihood that the change will succeed

l) Ref #6.13 - Are stakeholders hearing about problems with the Change from people outside the Change Team?

- All stakeholders must receive updates (regardless of whether they are good, bad or neutral) from the Change Team. Otherwise, the Change Team could lose control of what is happening which will cause problems with creditability, incorrect information being spread and inappropriate messaging for specific stakeholder groups.
- This will result in real challenges in implementing any change successfully.
- If this is happening the Change Manager (possibly with Sponsor support) will need to determine why this is happening and take immediate actions to stop it from continuing.

m) Ref #6.14 - How well are the external suppliers being managed?

- All organizations rely on external suppliers to provide a part of their service
- This means if a change needs to be made then these external suppliers will need to be involved and make a change themselves.
- To maximise the likelihood of change success, external suppliers must be managed effectively.
- There is a long list of change failures caused by poor external supplier management.
- This means that if any problems are identified then they need to be managed immediately.

n) Ref #6.15 - How well are intragroup or internal suppliers being managed?

- All organizations (especially medium and large ones) rely on intragroup suppliers to provide a part of their operating model.
- These intragroup suppliers could be spread across different locations, parts of the organisation, time zones, etc. They could also work in many different methods.
- This means if a change needs to be made then it will need to involve these intragroup suppliers.
- Therefore any involved intragroup suppliers must be managed effectively when a change is being
- There is a long list of change failures caused by poor intragroup supplier management.
- This means that if any problems are identified then they need to be managed immediately.

o) Ref #6.16 - How effectively are customers being managed?

- If clients are materially impacted by a change then they need to be involved in the change.
- Customers can be either external or internal.
- The poor management of clients is a key contributor to change failure.
- However, this can be complicated if the client needs to make major changes and/or there is a poor relationship between the organisation and the client(s).
- This means clients need to be involved quickly as possible to ensure they (a) understand the background to the change and (b) know what they need to change.
- This involvement will need to be supported by a robust two-way communication process
- Finally, it is important that any issues encountered are escalated to the Sponsor, Steering Committee and the senior management who manage the client relationship. This should hopefully reduce the change of change failure and negatively impact the client relationship.

p) Ref #6.17 - How well are the human aspects of the change being managed?

- If any human-related aspect issues are noticed then they need to be addressed immediately otherwise it will (a) cause issues with the change and (b) be very uncomfortable for the staff impacted.
- Therefore the Change Manager will need to ensure they are aware of any problems so the cause can be identified and the problems resolved.
- At all times, the Steering Committee, Sponsor and other relevant Senior Management need to be kept updated

q) Ref #6.18 - Remember that all changes will have issues and problems.

- Change is a complex subject and despite having the best plans in place there will be problems.
- Therefore, to manage expectations, all senior management must be aware of this.

r) Ref #6.19 - Is the change experiencing scope creep?

- One of the key causes for change problems or failures is scope creep.
- Therefore organisations and Change Teams need to ensure that all scope changes (without fail) are processed through the change Control process.
- This will ensure that there is a sufficient process in place to make sure any requests are fully assessed so that the relevant senior stakeholders can decide whether to approve or reject them.

s) Ref #6.20 - How paranoid is the Change Team about issues and problems?

- Change is complex and things can alter without the Change Team being aware of them. This can cause problems with implementation.
- This means the Change Manager (and team) need to be very paranoid about things going wrong and changing.
- They need to constantly re-review the change regularly to trap any problems.
- Remember only the paranoid deliver change

t) **Ref #6.21 - Are staff comfortable raising issues and/ or problems without the threat of repercussions from management or other colleges?**

• It is important the Change Team members (and other key staff) feel comfortable to raise issues and problems without fear of punishment.
• Otherwise, problems will not be addressed which could impact whether the Change is successful or not.
• If the Change Manager feels that people are uncomfortable about raising issues then they need to work with the impacted individuals on a 1-2-1 basis to (a) allow them to raise problems anonymously so (b) they can be addressed and managed.

u) **Ref #6.22 - Is the Change Team being appreciated for their work and efforts?**

• Changes can be stressful especially if team members are working long hours and/or there is a constant wave of issues.
• The senior stakeholders need to appreciate the efforts and achievements of the Change Team.
• It makes the team feel appreciated and it also motivates them for the future.
• Therefore senior stakeholders should be aware of the efforts of the Change Team and the achievements and send out "thank you" or "well done" messages to the relevant team members as appropriate.
• Finally, it is a good idea to tell the manager of Change Team members that they have performed a good job.

v) **Ref #6.23 - Remember to keep checking whether the triggers, business case, benefits, etc. are still valid?**

• It is important to constantly review all changes in progress

to ensure their triggers for change, business cases, etc. are still valid.
- It is possible that during the implementation of a change, there could be alternations in the external environment or the organisation alters itself that could invalidate the triggers, business case, etc.
- If so either the change needs to be updated to reflect this or terminated. Otherwise, the change will be a failure.

A.4 - Has sufficient preparation been performed for the go-live transition?

a) Ref #7.2 - Has everything been delivered that is needed for transition? (And what are the impacts of any gaps).

- Despite the best efforts of the Change Team and other related stakeholders, not everything will be ready at the transition date.
- While this can be frustrating annoying, it is a part of managing and implementing successful change and these situations need to be managed appropriately. If they are not managed then it can result in confusion, frustration, errors, and even possible change failure.
- Therefore all stakeholders must be aware of these gaps in delivery, the immediate impact when the change transitions into live, how these gaps will be managed in the interim and how they will be fixed long term.

b) Ref #7.3 - Is everything that needs to be transitioned into live working as planned?

- It is important to have a clear understanding that everything

due to be transitioned into the production environment is working as planned.
- This understanding of defects will allow (a) their impact to be assessed (b) any mitigations to be designed (c) long term fix plan to be devised so (c) the Sponsor, Steering Committee and other Senior Management can take an informed and proactive decision on whether to transition the change into production or wait until a later date.
- Transitioning a change into production with unknown or unmanaged defects will cause problems and could result in a change failure.

c) Ref #7.4 - Has a Transition Coordinator been nominated?

- To ensure a transition (and roll back if required) is completed successfully then a single person needs to be employed and be accountable to the Steering Committee and Sponsor to ensure the transition is completed
- This person is called the Transition Coordinator and their role covers are ensuring (a) all the pre-transition work is completed (such as planning, testing, etc.) (b) actual transition activity and, if necessary, roll-back activity is completed and (c) all post-transition activity is managed such as ensuring any problems or issues raised are managed to a close.
- This role should be filled as early as possible.
- If this person is not in place then the Transition could fail which will cause issues with the change and the wider organisation. (Although sometimes the Change Manager will perform this role).
- It may be necessary to use several different (sub) Transitions Coordinators to focus on specific areas and disciplines but these people will need to report to the main Transition Coordinator to ensure there is control, focus and accountability.

d) Ref #7.5 - Has the transition approach been agreed upon?

- By this stage of the change (i.e. pre-transition planning) then it is essential that the approach has been confirmed and agreed upon with required stakeholders
- If there is still any uncertainty or lack of agreement then this is a major issue and needs to be addressed by the Change Team and wider stakeholders immediately.
- No transition planning (let alone the actual transition itself) should start until an approach is crystal clear and agreed with all required stakeholders.
- Otherwise, not only with the change probably fail, but a failed or poorly thought through transitions could materially impact all aspects of the business.

e) Ref #7.6 - Is everybody aware that the transition is going to take place?

- Transitions events may need certain services to be temporality closed (such as losing a website for a weekend or not being able to trade in the evenings).
- All stakeholders either within or external to the organisation must be aware of any possible outages because (a) it will cause material problems and (b) they will need to make temporary arrangements
- This means that there needs to be a structured communication process to ensure all relevant people are made aware with sufficient notice.

f) Ref #7.7 - Is there clear ownership of the change before it is transitioned into live?

- All changes must have a pre-agreed owner before they go live

- If there is no owner before go-live then this should be escalated to the Sponsor and Steering Committee immediately for resolution.
- No change should transition into live unless there is a clear owner.

g) Ref #7.8 - Has sufficient training been performed before go-live?

- All changes require some sort of process change or alternation.
- Therefore, for a change to be successful then all staff (cover internal teams, suppliers and customers) must be trained in these changes and know how to use them when everything goes live.
- This will ensure that all processes, policies and procedures are updated.
- If they are not trained then it will cause problems and the change will not be successful.

h) Ref #7.9 - Is there a robust transition plan in place?

- A transition event must be planned in as much detail as possible otherwise there will be problems
- This plan should be driven by the Transition Coordinator.
- Poor transition management is a reason for change failure. It would be a real shame to perform all the earlier parts of the change perfectly but slip up on this final part
- The transition plan contains many parts namely some type of a list of the tasks to complete the transition, the required people to perform the work and sufficient controls and checks
- It is important to understand the "Point of no return". This is the latest time that any rollback plan can be started to ensure that all rollback activity is completed in time to minimise any

impact generally across the organisation.
- It is also important to think about what things could go wrong and ensure there are fall-back or contingency plans in place.
- If the Change Manager is encountering any issues with collating the plan then they must be escalated to the Sponsor, Steering Committee and other senior management.

i) Ref #7.10 - Is there a sufficient rollback plan in place?

- All transition events and plans must be accompanied by a set of roll-back plans to cover all the types of problems that could be encountered.
- This plan must exist so that any transition can be rolled back in the event of problems. Imagine the disastrous situation if change started to transition into live but failed and it was not possible to roll back to the original position?
- The Transition Manager should be responsible for completing the roll-back plan.
- The roll-back plan contains many parts namely some type of a list of the tasks to complete the transition, the required people to perform the work and sufficient controls and checks
- If the Change Manager is encountering any issues with collating the roll-back plan then they must be escalated to the Sponsor, Steering Committee and other senior management.

j) Ref #7.11 - Have both the transition and rollback plans been tested (both separately and together)?

- All transition and roll-back plans need to be tested thoroughly both separately and together.
- This testing is required to ensure that the plans are fit-for-purpose.
- The Transition Coordinator should ensure the testing is completed.

- It would be extremely risky to proceed with any type of transition without a set of fully and thoroughly tested transition and rollback plans. This is because there would be
- If the Change Manager is encountering any issues with collating the roll-back plan then they must be escalated to the Sponsor, Steering Committee and other senior management.

k) Ref #7.12 - Is the Change Team being appreciated for their work and efforts?

- Changes can be stressful especially if team members are working long hours and/or there is a constant wave of issues.
- The senior stakeholders need to appreciate the efforts and achievements of the Change Team.
- It makes the team feel appreciated and it also motivates them for the future.
- Therefore senior stakeholders should be aware of the efforts of the Change Team and the achievements and send out "thank you" or "well done" messages to the relevant team members as appropriate.

A.5 - Care is still required during the actual transition event

a) Ref #8.2 - Issues and problems will happen so prepare for them and a cool head is needed to manage them.

- All change transition events will have problems despite the amount of testing and preparation performed
- Therefore the Change Team and other involved stakeholders (such as the Sponsor and Change Manager) need to beware are of this so they are mentally prepared.

- If problems are encountered then they need to manage with a 'cool head' to ensure no poor decisions are made which result in a change failure or wider organisational issues.

b) Ref #8.3 - Follow the pre-agreed transition and rollbacks plan and only diverge from them with extreme caution.

- Before any transition into a live environment is executed then a set of transition and rollback plans should have been developed and tested.
- These plans should provide comfort that the change can be transitioned to and rolled back if required
- Therefore Change Teams should only diverge from these plans in extreme circumstances (such as major unforeseen problems).
- But if it is necessary to change the plan then the plan alterations, their impact and associated risks need to be understood and signed off by the Sponsor, Steering Committee and (if necessary) the clients and suppliers.

c) Ref #8.4 - Do not skip the control points within the transitions and roll-back plans.

- All transition and roll-back plans will have a series of controls points to (a) ensure that the plan is progressing as intended and (b) to provide an indication of problems
- These are in place to control and change the transition, change and the Change Team so they must not be skipped or ignored.
- There is unfortunately a long history of changes that ignored transition and rollback control points which meant issues were not trapped and/or managed and meant the change ultimately failed.

d) Ref #8.5 - Do not forget the point of no return.

- The "Point of No Return" is the latest date/time that a rollback can start to ensure that (a) the failed transition plan can be reversed and (b) the wider organisation is not impacted adversely by this failed transition.
- Therefore this point needs to be monitored proactively to ensure that stakeholders are aware when this date/time is near or passed so they can make any required decisions on whether to start a roll-back.

e) Ref #8.6 - Is the Change Team being appreciated for their work and efforts?

- Changes can be stressful especially if team members are working long hours and/or there is a constant wave of issues.
- The senior stakeholders need to appreciate the efforts and achievements of the Change Team.
- It makes the team feel appreciated and it also motivates them for the future.
- Therefore senior stakeholders should be aware of the efforts of the Change Team and the achievements and send out "thank you" or "well done" messages to the relevant team members as appropriate.

A.6 - Remember that all changes need a certain amount of post-implementation support.

a) Ref #9.2 - Are all stakeholders aware that change takes time to bed in and this will mean the Change Team needs to be kept in place (often at a cost).

- All changes required a certain amount of bedding in post-transition.

- Therefore the Change Team (or parts of it) must be kept in place to provide any support required for a pre-agreed period
- All senior stakeholders will need to be aware of this because apart from (a) tying up the Change Team and stopping them from working on new initiatives or even being let go, it will (b) incur a cost for the organisation and possibly any impacted suppliers and customers.

b) Ref #9.3 - Is there are a clear set of handover criteria to pass the ownership of change from the Change Team to the required business teams?

- While it is noted that the Change Team will need to support the transition change in the period just after go-live, the Change Team cannot support the change forever.
- This is because it is costly, the Change Team may be required for other changes (or even let go if they are expensive consultants) and, ultimately, the business teams need to own the change at some point.
- This means that a clear set of handover criteria needs to be agreed upon to determine when and how the change will pass from the Change Team to the business owners. If this criterion is not clear then it could result in confusion over ownership which could result in change failure.

c) Ref #9.4 - Is the Change Team being appreciated for their work and efforts?

- Changes can be stressful especially if team members are working long hours and/or there is a constant wave of issues.
- The senior stakeholders need to appreciate the efforts and achievements of the Change Team.
- It makes the team feel appreciated and it also motivates them for the future.

- Therefore senior stakeholders should be aware of the efforts of the Change Team and the achievements and send out "thank you" or "well done" messages to the relevant team members as appropriate.

A.7 There is still work to do even though the change is complete

a) Ref #10.2 - Was the change been successful or not?

- Once a change is completed then it needs to be assessed to understand whether it was successful or not.
- This can be done by reviewing the key success criteria to determine whether they have been met or not.
- If there are any gaps where the success criteria have not been met then it is important (a) to understand the reasons why (b) to understand the impact of these criteria not being met and then (c) to agree on how they should be managed going forward. Any decision made will need approval from the Sponsor, Steering Committee and possibly other senior management, customers and suppliers

b) Ref #10.3 - Has a post-implementation review of the lessons learnt exercise been completed?

- One of the key reasons for change failure (and organisational problems generally) is not learning from their mistakes and then repeating the same mistakes continually.
- Therefore, when a change is completed, some type of lessons learned or post-implementation review needs to be completed.
- When the output of this review is available then any

lessons or recommendations fed back must be fed back into the organisation's processes, procedures and behaviours to ensure they 'stick' and the issues are not repeated on future changes.

c) Ref #10.4 - Have all the successes been celebrated?

- There is a tendency to focus on issues and problems when a change has been implemented
- However, it is important to celebrate any success to ensure that people's efforts are recognised, that they appreciated and to ensure they are motivated them going forward.
- Therefore when a change completes then the Sponsor, Change Manager and other senior management need to thank the team for their efforts.
- There are various options regarding how this can be done ranging from a simple 'thank you' email to a large social event. However, any recognition needs to ensure it fits in with the culture of the Change Team and the organisation.

d) Ref #10.5 - Has the change been formally closed?

- When a change completes then a formal change closure report should be completed which will trigger the end of the change.
- This document will need to contain lessons learnt, gaps in the success criteria and a list of who owns the completion of any outstanding task.
- This document would also need to be formally approved and signed off by the Steering Committee and Sponsor.
- Also as part of this closure phase, there needs to be some housekeeping where all documents, emails, reports, etc. need to be stored in a central repository to allow easy access if required in the future.

www.ingramcontent.com/pod-product-compliance
Lightning Source LLC
Chambersburg PA
CBHW070641120526
44590CB00013BA/817